PHILOSOPHY OF MIND A–Z

T0386724

Volumes available in the Philosophy A–Z Series

Forthcoming volumes

Philosophy of Mind A–Z

Marina Rakova

Edinburgh University Press

In memory of Galina Alexeevna Makashova,
teacher and friend

© Marina Rakova, 2006

Edinburgh University Press Ltd
22 George Square, Edinburgh

Typeset in 10.5/13 Sabon
by TechBooks, India, and printed and
bound in Great Britain by
The Cromwell Press, Trowbridge, Wilts

A CIP record for this book is
available from the British Library

ISBN-10 0 7486 2215 2 (hardback)
ISBN-13 978 0 7486 2215 3 (hardback)
ISBN-10 0 7486 2095 8 (paperback)
ISBN-13 978 0 7486 2095 1 (paperback)

The right of Marina Rakova
to be identified as author of this work
has been asserted in accordance with
the Copyright, Designs and Patents Act 1988.

Contents

Series Editor's Preface

The philosophy of mind is one of those areas of philosophy that has a close connection with science. The precise nature of that connection is unclear, though, and we tend to think that abstract issues in philosophy are independent of scientific developments and discoveries. Yet the progress that takes place in the understanding of the nature of the mind on a scientific level clearly has an impact on the philosophical discussion, not in the sense of coming down on one rather than on another side of an argument, but because science continues to frame the arguments in different ways. The familiar problems such as how the body and the mind are connected, and what is meant by consciousness, for example, are often now articulated in terms of contemporary scientific understandings of the mind and action. The very modern issue of how far we can talk of machines thinking is a good example of how the nature of the mind and what it means to be a thinking thing resonates through the centuries to become particularly acute in an age that is familiar with artificial intelligence. Almost all the major philosophers had something, usually a great deal, to say on the philosophy of mind, and their positions have been briefly but accurately outlined in this book. Philosophy of mind has today become one of the most difficult areas of philosophy with a technical vocabulary of its own, perhaps due to its links with the science of the mind, and Marina Rakova has done us all a service in providing a clear and comprehensive guide to the terminology.

Oliver Leaman

Introduction

In one form or another, philosophy of mind has always been a major area of philosophical inquiry, although it is only in the last century, when the so-called mind–body problem began to be tackled head on, that it achieved the spectacular prominence it continues to enjoy today. This special placement of philosophy of mind in our intellectual endeavours is not surprising: there invariably comes a point when understanding the nature of the outer reality requires turning an inquiring eye to the nature of the mind. One could argue that this trend marks all the major periods in the history of philosophy, but it will be sufficient to note how much it has resurfaced in recent years. Other disciplines within philosophy, such as epistemology, metaphysics or ethics, are becoming more and more closely concerned with mental properties, and scientific publications no longer shun the problem of consciousness or that of the evolution of mentality as of merely speculative interest.

This makes it all the more difficult to outline the exact province of the philosophy of mind and select only those entries for inclusion in a dictionary that properly belong to it. My approach was to reflect in as much detail as possible the main issues occupying today the community of mind and cognition researchers and provide the historical background essential for understanding them (like the unwaning influence of Descartes on modern thought or the present relevance of the medieval problem of universals). However, I also judged it necessary to go beyond what may be seen as properly philosophical problem areas and include in this dictionary some crucial empirical terms and issues of which anyone interested in the philosophy of mind should be aware (such as the landmarks of vision research, scientific explanations of consciousness or discussions surrounding the neuron doctrine).

Overall, what I wanted to produce was the kind of dictionary that I would myself have enjoyed having at my side when first making inroads into the philosophy of mind. Thus I have included here some high-currency phrases which one invariably comes across in the literature but which are often left unexplained to the puzzlement of readers new to the area (for example, 'Cartesian theatre' or 'exaptation'). However, I thought it would be wrong to merely provide their definitions without placing them into the broad contexts where they make their appearance, which is why entries for such terms refer the reader for their explanation to other articles (for the examples given these are, respectively, 'self, the' and 'evolution').

I also placed special emphasis on explaining the ambiguity present in some important and frequent terms (for example, 'representationalism', 'property dualism' or even 'functionalism'). There is an opinion that such ambiguity is endemic to philosophy. Be that as it may, it is certainly baffling to someone who is new to the philosophy of mind. All such considerations added up to form the main principle behind the choice of entries for this dictionary: to help the student or any interested layperson to get a quick grasp of some unfamiliar territory and become 'unbaffled'. Finally, as regards the structuring of the entries themselves, I made a special point of not only providing their precise definitions and answering the question 'what it is' but of also answering the question 'why it matters', which is one of the first questions an inquisitive person asks when confronted with a new problem area.

I realise only too well that some readers are bound to question my choice of entries, either doubting the appropriateness of some of them in a philosophy of mind dictionary or lamenting the absence of their favourite thinkers. Making the final decision on what potential entries can be omitted, given the space limitations, was in itself a task of soul-tearing proportions, but that decision had to be made. I have stated here some of the criteria that determined the ultimate selection of entries for this dictionary and I hope that the reader will find this volume helpful and easy to use.

Acknowledgements

I most sincerely wish to thank:

The Series Editor, Oliver Leaman, for getting me involved in this complicated but ultimately rewarding project. He came up with the brilliant idea of producing these very timely and handy philosophy guides, and I hope he will be pleased with what he is going to get.

The two anonymous reviewers for Edinburgh University Press whose comments were most useful in making me recall that philosophy of mind is not confined to those particular areas of it that I am interested in myself. Unfortunately it proved impossible to squeeze all their suggestions into this slim book.

Members of psyche-D e-mail discussion list (especially Andrew Brook, Steven Lehar, Eric Dietrich and Mitch Gunzler) for their clarifications and debates which migrated into this volume in disguise. Michael Beaney, Elena Sviridova and Natalia Dobreytina also helped me with various bits and pieces.

Andrew Brook, Timothy Williamson and James R. Hurford for kindly reading some of my entries for me and letting me know whenever something struck them as strange, imprecise or downright wrong. And, of course, their comments in themselves were a pleasure to read.

xii   ACKNOWLEDGEMENTS

Everyone else whose ideas I might have stolen without explicitly acknowledging the fact. I would certainly have done so if I had had another ten thousand words of elbow room to manoeuvre in. As a model of a reader-friendly dictionary I used Simon Blackburn's *The Oxford Dictionary of Philosophy* (Oxford University Press, 1996).

All the students I have ever taught and who have taught me that things have to be both clear and informative, and that this is the only way.

Andrew M. Tune for reducing my teaching load a little while I was writing this.

Carol Macdonald from Edinburgh University Press for delicately taking control over my poor time management skills and getting this volume into production, and Peter Williams for kindly attending to my last minute whims and making sure they find their way into the final version of the text.

My father Boris Rakov and my brother Dmitry Rakov for their emotional and technical support.

My partner Denis Gladkov, my dearest and strictest critic, who never failed to let me know if something was unclear to him. If he had not been around for me to lean on his shoulder, which he patiently bore, I would never have completed this book. Now that it is over, I hope he will be able to get some life.

And of course we both thank our cat Kosha for providing me with inspiration. Cats are very philosophical animals. It is a pity, though, that they do not think much of our, that is humans', kind of minds.

Marina Rakova

Philosophy of Mind A–Z

A

Abduction: the notion introduced by **Peirce** to classify syllogisms of the type: (1) As are Bs; (2) Cs are Bs; (3) therefore, Cs are As. Although this form of reasoning is formally fallacious, Peirce viewed it as pertaining to scientific discovery. Abductive reasoning is also characteristic of our everyday reasoning as inference to the best explanation on the basis of limited evidence. Being non-algorithmic, which is not easily formalisable through the application of a set of rules, sensitive to context and one's overall knowledge, it presents problems for the **computational theory of mind**.

Ability Hypothesis see **Knowledge-how**

Absent *Qualia:* an argument against **functionalism** originated by Ned Block. If there can be a system identical to humans in functional organisation but lacking subjective experience, then the nature of *qualia* is not functional. The China-body system ('Chinese nation', 'Chinese gym'), where a billion people send radio commands to each other and an artificial body realising your functional organisation, is one such example. A possible response is that it is logically impossible for a state without **phenomenal** character to be functionally identical to a state possessing such character (they will differ with respect to phenomenal beliefs they give rise to).

Access Consciousness (a-consciousness): a kind of **consciousness** distinguished by Ned Block from **phenomenal consciousness** (p-consciousness) or experience. A **representation** is a-conscious if it is available for free use in reasoning and rational control of behaviour (including verbal reports). The distinction is motivated by the need to accommodate **consciousness** within the **computational theory of mind**. Thus, a-consciousness is a functional or **information**-processing correlate of p-consciousness (which requires a biological solution). To show that they are distinct kinds Block considers cases where they come apart. P-consciousness without a-consciousness is present when, for example, involved in a conversation you keep raising your voice without realising that you do so because of some loud noise outside: you are p-conscious, but not a-conscious of the noise. And an example of a-consciousness without p-consciousness would be obtained if **blindsight** subjects could prompt themselves to identify objects presented to them. A-consciousness without p-consciousness is characteristic of **zombies,** and to avoid their possibility Block admits that a-consciousness must be parasitic on p-consciousness. Block's approach, shared by several philosophers, is called the *bifurcated view*: it considers **phenomenal** states as functional but also defends **realism** about *qualia*.

Further reading: Block (1995a)

Accidental Property (contingent property): a property which an individual or kind could have failed to have without ceasing to be what it essentially is (for example, 'being a student').

Acquaintance see **Russell, Bertrand**

Action: that which an agent does rather than a mere physical rearrangement of one's body parts. Actions are carried out with certain **intentions,** and this links the notions of action and **agency** to those of **rationality** and **intentionality.** According to the *causal theory of action*, associated with **Hume** but already found in **Aristotle,** *intentional action* needs desire to provide goals and belief as a means of potentially achieving them. However, there arises the problem of **mental causation** (*reasons and causes*): it seems that as we act for reasons, action must be explained in terms of reasons, which is not a kind of causal explanation. This approach, characteristic of Wittgensteinean theories of action such as **Anscombe**'s, was questioned by **Davidson** who argued that reasons must have physical bases, and thus be efficacious in causing action (for otherwise one should not think of them as reasons at all). But if one holds that an action must be explained in terms of its immediate cause, one may miss important generalisations. This is the idea of *basic action*: although one phones one's parents by dialling their number and does that by hitting buttons on the telephone and so on, all the subsequent descriptions seem inadequate to explain one's action (the problem of action **individuation**). A similar point was made by Christopher Peacocke and Timothy Williamson against those versions of **internalism** which view actions as bodily movements caused by internal states individuated without reference to the agent's environment. **Intentional states** guiding even such simple actions as crossing a road cannot be factorised into internal and external components because many actions involve deliberation (are not instantaneous) and require constant feedback from the environment. The notion of action was also recently employed to question the classical notion of mental **representation** (see **embedded cognition**).

Further reading: Davidson (1980); Mele (1997)

Adaptation: a characteristic of an organism which arose through **evolution** by natural selection.

Adaptationism (Neo-Darwinism): the view that natural selection is the main driving force of **evolution**. However, the term is often reserved for the controversial view that most characteristics of organisms are **adaptations** that enhance organisms' survival and can be explained in terms of genes' tendency to proliferation. For this reason, adaptationist explanations are sometimes pejoratively labelled 'just so stories' and 'the Panglossian paradigm', evoking, respectively, Rudyard Kipling's children's stories and Voltaire's Dr Pangloss (*Candide*) who believed that ours is the best of all possible worlds. Adaptationism is particularly controversial as an explanation of the evolution of human **cognition** in that it commits the **teleological** fallacy of holding that every psychological feature is an optimal solution to some design problem posed by an organism's environment, and tends to assume step-by-step continuity between features of increasing complexity (**evolutionary psychology**). The **teleological theory of content** explores the role of natural selection in establishing representational **content** of **intentional states** (beliefs, desires). **Dennett**, who holds that the **intentional stance** applies to organisms only when they reach a certain level of complexity, argues that all intentionality can be derived from the intentionality of natural selection (the notion of 'selection for'). But this view is problematic because it imbues natural selection with sensitivity to **intensional** distinctions and the capacity to be directed toward non-existent entities, which cannot be properties of natural selection understood as a purely physical phenomenon.

Further reading: Dennett (1995)

Adverbialism: a theory of **perception** (primarily **vision**) which appeared in the mid-1940s as a reaction against the **sense-datum theory**. It holds that there are only modifications of our experience which, to avoid the error of **reification** (positing **sense-data**), should be described with the help of adverbial modifiers, saying, for example, that one is appeared to green-squarely instead of saying that one sees a green square. However, such descriptions are problematic for more complex visual scenes, and the nature of modified states cannot be understood without reference to objects of experience. Today, adverbialism is popular among proponents of subjectivism about **colour** because it allows one to say that mental colours are identical with or supervenient on neural states while avoiding commitment to **mental objects**. Adverbial analyses are also applied to **propositional attitudes** to avoid commitment to propositions as peculiar objects in one's **ontology**.

Further reading: Chisholm (1957); Tye (1989)

Affordance see **Direct Perception**

Agency: being in control of or responsible for one's **actions**.

Analytic Functionalism (conceptual, common-sense, causal role functionalism): the variety of **functionalism** which stems from **Lewis's** analysis of psychological terms. Unlike **machine functionalism**, analytic functionalism supports *type* **physicalism** holding that a **mental state** can be analysed into a *role state* (its role in the explanation of behaviour) and a *realiser state* (the underlying physical state which accounts for its causal properties). Analytic functionalists also accept Lewis's approach to mental **representation** inspired by Ramsey's view of beliefs as 'maps by which we steer'. It opposes the **language of thought** hypothesis by holding that mental representation is like representation in geographical maps: structured, systematic, containing a finite amount of **information**, but continuous. This follows from the **holism** of the mental: because beliefs and desires are attributed to subjects *en masse* on the basis of their behavioural **dispositions** and considerations of **rationality**, the whole system of beliefs is the fundamental unit of **content**, and the content of individual beliefs can be stated only approximately. However, it is not clear whether representation in maps is non-discrete and whether the approach can meet the **compositionality** constraint. Besides, it needs to address the problems of content holism, **indeterminacy** and belief under **entailment**.

Further reading: Braddon-Mitchell and Jackson (1996)

Ancient Philosophy (approximately 600 BC – AD 400): emerging as an inquiry about the natural world, pre-Socratic philosophy tied the question of what distinguishes appearance from reality (**ontology**) to that of the nature of **knowledge**. Thus Parmenides of Elea (*c*.510–451 BC) held that true Being is unchanging and can be grasped only by reason, concluding that sensible appearances do not exist. In Athens, Anaxagoras (*c*.500–428 BC) resolved Parmenides' puzzle about the impossibility of change by viewing matter as a flow of qualities rather than some extended stuff supporting them and originated the conception of cosmic *Nous* (reason, intellect) which sets matter in motion and of which humans have the largest share (arguably the first version of **dualism**). Democritus of Abdera (*c*.460–370 BC) first raised the question about the

relationship between sense-**perception** and reason, concluding that only reason can deliver knowledge of the
essence of reality. He was also the first defender of **materialism**, holding that, like everything else, human *psyche* is made of atom combinations (*psyche*, translated as
'soul', did not mean 'the conscious **self**' but rather 'life-
principle', necessary but not sufficient for **consciousness**
and thought). **Plato** and **Aristotle** then defined the subsequent development of much Western philosophy. Of
interest are also the three schools that appeared after
Aristotle's death: Stoicism with its theory of *phantasia
kataleptike* (apprehensive perception delivering knowledge of reality) and the first **cognitive** theory of **emotions**
(Chrysippus, *c*.280–207 BC), Epicureanism with its combination of atomism and subjectivism about secondary
qualities like **colour**, and **Scepticism**.
   Further reading: Annas (1992)

Animal Cognition: the way non-human animals process **information** about their natural environments studied by
cognitive ethology. Interest in animal **cognition** has always been marked by the dichotomy of continuity and
discontinuity in cognitive capacities of human and non-
human animals and the search for distinguishing human
characteristics (such as possession of reason according to
Aristotle or **Kant**). Many recent discussions were marked
by differing stands on the **Cartesian** view of animals as
automata to whom the ascription of **minds** or **consciousness** is unnecessary. Because animals exhibit no flexibility in response to novel situations, voluntary **action** or
creative use of language, **Descartes** thought that their behaviour can be given a purely mechanistic explanation.
This view is especially pronounced in a common equa-
tion of **thought** with **language** possession which provoked
many investigations aiming to prove that linguistic capacities of non-human animals are continuous with those of

humans. Such studies often explicitly opposed **Chomsky's** views on the uniqueness of the human faculty of language (FL), but more recently, in collaboration with cognitive ethologists, Chomsky proposed that FL characterised by **recursive** syntax has a predecessor in 'the faculty of language in the broad sense' which includes a conceptual-intentional system and the computational mechanisms of recursion evolved for dealing with navigation and social relations. Recognising our continuity with non-human animals provides new perspectives on the problems of **representation** (their capacity to correct perceptual errors), orders of **intentionality** (**theory of mind**), **phenomenal consciousness** in its relation with intentionality (thus multimodal integration is present in mammals but is absent in the reptilian line) and **self-consciousness**.

Further reading: Savage-Rumbaugh et al. (1998); Hauser et al. (2002)

Animalism see **Personal identity**

Anomalous Monism: the position advocated by **Davidson** that although all events are physical events (hence **monism**), **mental properties** cannot be identified with physical properties. To allow for **mental causation** Davidson accepts the identity of **mental events** with physical events (causal relations exist only between events that enter into **causal laws**) and the dependence (**supervenience**) of the mental on the physical. However, he holds that there are no strict laws to connect mental and physical events. The ascription of **mental states** to a person is **holistic** (a whole bunch of mental states must be ascribed to someone in order to explain a piece of their behaviour) and guided by considerations of **normativity** and **rationality**. And although an event may have a physical and a mental description, because of the radically different natures of our mental and physical predicates (holistic versus discrete) it is a priori impossible to formulate laws connecting them. **Mental concepts** are 'unsuited' to laws, and only ontological but not conceptual **reduction** is possible. Davidson was charged with **epiphenomenalism** because having a mental description does not seem to affect the causal powers of an event. His reply was that for causal powers, unlike for laws, the nature of descriptions is irrelevant, but it remains unclear whether this explains the causal efficacy of the mental qua mental.

Further reading: Davidson (1970)

Anscombe, G. Elizabeth M. (1919–2001): British philosopher, an authority on **Wittgenstein**. Anscombe anticipated many current ideas about **action, intentionality** and **perception**. She also criticised the **Cartesian** way of thinking about the first-person pronoun as referring to the immutable **self**.

Further reading: Anscombe (1957)

Apperception see **Self-consciousness**

Aquinas, St Thomas (1225–74): Dominican theologian and philosopher. Aquinas sought to reconcile faith and reason through **Aristotle**'s solution to the problem of **universals**. From him **Brentano** got the notion of **intentionality** as 'inexistence': a cloud you saw a few minutes ago may not exist any more, but you can have it in your **mind** because you have the **concept** (*intentio*) of cloud. Aquinas also developed Aristotle's views on the soul, holding that being a **person** requires the unity of the soul with the body, because otherwise the images on which personal **memory** depends would be lost. He defended genuine human **agency** against Augustinianism and **occasionalism**, and denied **privileged access** holding that **knowledge** of our own **mental states** is the result of abstraction.

Further reading: Aquinas (2001)

Aristotle (the Philosopher, 384–322 BC): Ancient Greek philosopher, the creator of **logic** and most scientific divisions. Aristotle rejected **Plato**'s forms (**universals**) as existing outside things by adopting Plato's own argument that if one takes a set of two particulars sharing the form, one then gets a set consisting of the two particulars and the form, and must find a further form unifying them, which leads to infinite regress ('the third man argument'). He proposed instead that universals exist in things, which accords with his analysis of *substance* as that which persists through change in its accidents (**accidental properties**). However, for Aristotle, a substance is both matter and form: thus, a wax stamp is only that when matter is given a particular form. Similarly, a human being cannot be divided into the soul and the body, because the soul is the body's form. As for Aristotle **knowledge** requires some similarity between the knower and the knowable, corporeal beings must begin with sense **perception**. But the highest part of the soul, the intellect, is immortal and immaterial because otherwise it could not contemplate all the forms abstracted from perception. This fits well with Aristotle's four-dimensional analysis of causality (and hence, an individual's or kind's identity) into material, formal, efficient (the agency effecting the result) and final (the *telos* or purpose for which something exists) causes, which is the first formulation of **functionalism** and **teleological** explanation. Aristotle's practical syllogism (the rule for acting on the basis of beliefs and desires) similarly anticipates the **representational theory of mind**.

   Further reading: Aristotle (1984)

Armstrong, David M. (b.1926): Australian philosopher, one of the originators of the **causal theory of mind**. Extending **Place**'s **identity theory** to beliefs and desires, he called his theory *Central State Materialism* because science finds causes of behaviour in the states of central nervous systems. He defended scientific **realism** about **universals** and **direct realism** about **perception**, and developed a **higher-order theory** of **consciousness**. His sympathies are still with **reductive physicalism** and he believes it a matter of scientific investigation to explain the deducibility of **mental properties** from physical properties.

Further reading: Armstrong (1968)

Artificial Intelligence (AI): the branch of computer science concerned with designing machines that could perform tasks which require **intelligence** from humans and that could accomplish them in less time and with greater reliability. Stemming from **Turing**'s insights, the field was shaped by John McCarthy, Marvin Minsky, Allen Newell and Herbert Simon. Following **Searle** one can distinguish between strong and weak AI. *Strong AI* holds that the right sort of computer program can literally do what human **minds** do, whereas *weak AI* only aims to develop computational models simulating human **cognitive** abilities. The status of strong AI remains controversial, but recent interest in **consciousness** and **embodiment** led to the extension of AI's traditional concerns towards awareness, **emotions** and **imagination**. The term AI (**GOFAI**) is sometimes used more narrowly to refer to the **computational theory of mind** as opposed to **connectionism**.

Aspectual Shape see **Searle, John R.**

Associationism (associationist psychology): the first empirical psychological theory anticipated by **Aristotle** and developed by **Locke**, **Hume**, David Hartley (1705–57), both **Mills** and Alexander Bain (1818–1903). Associationism aimed to discover general principles of thought in laws of association between **ideas**, which were identified as the laws of contiguity, similarity and contrast. Thus sensory impressions occurring together or in immediate succession (like the furriness, four-leggedness and barking of dogs) get associated and, because the **mind** operates by summing or subtracting images, thinking of furry creatures causes one to think of them as four-legged. Association laws were also studied by **introspective psychology** and, though not as laws of thought, by **methodological behaviourism** which supplanted associationism. Viewing **cognitive** processes in terms of causal interactions between ideas, associationism anticipated the **computational theory of mind**. Its analysis of ideas in terms of feature combinations is still central to the **prototype theory of concepts**. Its tenet that thinking reduces to generalisation from experience was resurrected by **connectionism** (after the discovery of the nerve cell in the 1890s, neural networks were contemplated by **James** and **Freud** as a biological vindication of associationism). However, as **Kant** and, later, **Chomsky** emphasised, thinking cannot be merely putting ideas into sequences but requires organising principles sensitive to hierarchical constituent structure.

See also: Pinker (2002)

Asymmetric Dependence: a version of the **informational theory of content** proposed by **Fodor** which tackles the **disjunction problem** without appeal to special types of situations. Asymmetric dependence is a metaphysically basic **content**-constituting condition formulated in terms of law-governed relations among properties. Thus CAT means *cat* and not *cat or dog* because the law connecting the property of being a dog and the property of being a cause of CAT tokenings asymmetrically depends on the law connecting the property of being a cat and the property of being a cause of CAT tokenings, so that if the law 'cat → cause of CAT' did not hold, the law 'dog → cause of CAT' would not hold either, but if the law 'dog → cause of CAT' did not hold, the law 'cat → cause of CAT' would hold anyway. To deal with **Twin-Earth** cases, the third condition states that some tokenings of a mental representation R must be actually caused by Rs.

Further reading: Fodor (1987)

Atomism: the view that the **content** of a **concept** does not depend on its relations with other concepts (see **informational atomism**).

Austin, John L. (1911–60): British linguistic philosopher, the originator of speech act theory. Austin's attack on the argument from **illusion**, whose soundness he questioned arguing that there are **phenomenal** differences between genuine **perception** and **hallucination**, made **Place** reject the **sense-datum theory**.

Further reading: Austin (1962)

Autism: a psychological disorder characterised by social withdrawal and severe communication difficulties; possibly an impairment of the **theory of mind** module (at the neural level it involves reduced cerebral flow and decreased metabolism of the prefrontal region).

Autonomy of Psychology see **Special Sciences**

Background, The: the notion introduced by **Searle** to designate a set of abilities, skills, **dispositions** and presuppositions which, being non-intentional, are necessary to 'ground' **intentional states**. It is not enough to analyse a belief together with other beliefs as does **functionalism**, because this analysis has to stop somewhere. For Searle, it stops at the simple ability to act in the world.

Further reading: Searle (1983)

Behaviourism: the view that possession of **mental states** should be identified with observable behaviour or behavioural **dispositions**: to be in a mental state (for example, to think that there is a tree in front of one) is to be disposed to behave in a certain way. The central thesis of **methodological** and **logical behaviourism** is the denial of internal representational states mediating behaviour.

Belief Box see **Language of Thought**

Belief-Desire Psychology see **Folk Psychology**

Berkeley, George (1685–1753): Irish philosopher, the originator of subjective **idealism**. If one separates the **mind** from matter (as does **Cartesian** substance **dualism**), then it becomes difficult to understand how the mind could acquire **knowledge** of the material world through **perception**. **Representationalism** confuses rather than clarifies matters: if what one knows is only an **idea**, one can never be sure that there is anything in the world corresponding to it, for the only way one could try to find that out is by forming another idea. Thus representationalism leads to **scepticism**, which Berkeley rejected. Instead, entertaining the possibility of total **illusion** and reintroducing the contact between mind and body through a **direct perception** thesis (we directly perceive what really exists), he concluded that everything exists in the mind only, that there is no material substance. To be is to be perceived (*esse est percipi*). This was established by Berkeley's *master* *argument*: one cannot conceive of a tree which is unconceived, what is conceived is in the mind, therefore there is nothing existing outside the mind. The world given to us in experience is the world of connections between particular ideas in their relation to their archetypes in the mind of God who created the world of ordinary objects inside the mental realm. (Note that Berkeley's brand of **empiricism** denies the existence of general ideas other than mere commonalities in naming.) Although subsequent philosophers were not convinced by Berkeley's argument feeling that it is a verbal trick, he raised important issues about the extent to which one can trust common sense.

Further reading: Berkeley (1975)

Binding Problem: the problem of explaining how **information** processed by different subsystems is integrated into unified perceptual **representations** within the same and across different sensory modalities. Thus representations of **colour**, shape, motion, etc. produced in different areas of visual cortex are integrated to give rise to visual experiences of distinct objects simultaneously having all such properties (temporal binding).

Biological Naturalism see **Searle, John R.**

Blindsight: the condition (cortical blindness resulting from the destruction of primary visual cortex) in which subjects have no experience of an object presented to their blind field (scotoma) and are incapable of identifying it. In Block's terms, they lack both **phenomenal** and **access consciousness**. However, they retain the ability to locate 'unseen' objects and discriminate between them if prompted to guess from a small number of alternatives. 'Affective blindsight' is the term for subjects' ability to discriminate emotional facial expressions presented to their blind fields in the absence of phenomenal visual awareness.

Brain: the part of the central nervous system contained in the skull. Many **philosophy of mind** issues involve reference to the brain's organisation and **cognitive** functioning, but the most pressing one is the **mind–body problem**. The belief that the **mind** and the brain are intimately connected gives rise to the locution 'the mind/ brain' (popularised by **Chomsky**). But the locution itself can be understood in several ways – is the mind that which the brain does? is the mind realised by the brain? is the mind the same as the brain? Another issue concerns the general debate in **cognitive science** surrounding the notions of **representation** and **computation** and, by extension, their application to the brain's functioning. In **neuroscience**, this is the issue surrounding the generally accepted *neuron doctrine*, the view that **neurons** are the brain's main computational-representational units. Some researchers argue that it ignores the importance of structures internal to the cell body (the cytoskeleton; simple but arguably cognitive functions can be performed by single-cell paramecia), the existence of extensive intra-dendritic **information** processing and non-synaptic dendro-dendritic communication, and the involvement of larger brain units in cognitive functions.

Further reading: Bear et al. (2001)

Brains in Vats (brain-in-a-bottle): a **thought experiment** in favour of **internalism** (and also indirect **representationalism**) intended to show that a **brain** put in a vat and electrically stimulated (or, in more recent versions, existing in virtual reality) will have a full mental life of thoughts and experiences while not receiving any input from the environment. The **scepticism** engendered by the experiment exploits our intuitions about the contingent character of **mind**–world relations.

Further reading: Putnam (1981)

Brentano, Franz (1838–1917): German philosopher who laid the foundations of contemporary **philosophy of mind** by reintroducing the notion of **intentionality** or the **mind**'s 'direction toward an object'. Today, any theory of intentionality must address *Brentano's problem*: how can **mental states** be about things? (*Brentano's thesis* is the view that **intentional states** are not reducible to physical states.) Brentano's own notion of intentionality, however, was importantly different from ours: for him, it was a property of phenomenally conscious mental acts which, apart from being directed to objects, are always directed to themselves as secondary objects.

Further reading: Brentano [1874] (1973)

Bridge Laws see **Nagelian Reduction**

Broad, C. D. see **Emergentism**

Broad Content (wide content): that **content** of **intentional states** (beliefs, desires, etc.) which constitutively depends on the external environment in which individuals having these states are embedded. Broadness is a property of many non-psychological states: whether a mark on the skin is a mosquito bite depends on there being a causal-historical connection between it and some mosquito (and not an evil person inflicting mosquito-bite imitations on people). In his **Twin-Earth** argument **Putnam** showed that thoughts about **natural kinds** have broad content (natural kind **externalism**). Tyler Burge extended Putnam's **essentialism** to all kinds of thoughts that depend on individuals' social environment (*social externalism*). In Burge's

thought experiment, a person, say Alf, suffers from arthritis and has several correct thoughts about his ailment (that he has suffered from arthritis for years, that certain aches are characteristic of arthritis, and so on). One day he decides that he also has arthritis in his thigh, but later learns from his doctor that he was mistaken because arthritis is an inflammation of joints. However, in a different **possible world** where doctors use the word 'arthritis' differently, Alf would have been right. Burge concludes that the content of Alf's **concept** ARTHRITIS depends on the linguistic practice of his community (it is a *deferential concept* for him). Proponents of **internalism** object that this interpretation unjustly ascribes to Alf (at least before he saw the doctor) two contradictory thoughts that arthritis is and is not an inflammation of joints. Thus his concept cannot be the same as the experts', and to make sense of Alf's beliefs we need to know their **narrow content.**

Further reading: Burge (1979)

Bundle Theory see **Self, The**

C Fibres see **Pain**

Carnap, Rudolf (1891–1970): German philosopher of **logical positivism.** Beginning with **phenomenalism,** Carnap later questioned the priority of experience and worked on the **unity of science.** Aiming towards philosophical clarification of scientific language, he distinguished between material and formal modes of speech and, in later work, between questions internal and external to certain linguistic frameworks. (Note the difference between asking whether someone is experiencing a blue after-image and asking whether there are **sense-data**.) He anticipated the **identity theory** (suggesting it as a linguistic recommendation) and the **language of thought** hypothesis (though he viewed **propositional attitudes** as relations to natural language sentences). He also anticipated **atomism**, suggesting that conceptual relations can be analysed in terms of *meaning postulates*: x is a bachelor → x is not married. Whereas for Carnap this was an analysis of analyticity in terms of consequences arising from linguistic conventions, it shows how **concepts** can be related in thought without being contained in one another.

Further reading: Carnap (1947)

Cartesian: relating to **Descartes'** philosophy.

Cartesian Theatre see **Self, The**

Cartesianism see **Rationalism**

Categorisation: the way organisms arrange stimuli into categories. **Cognitive psychology** uses two main tasks in the study of categorisation: *category identification* (when subjects are asked to identify the category to which an object belongs, for example say whether penguins are birds) and *category production* (when subjects are asked to name the attributes of some object or decide whether an object has a certain attribute).

Category Mistake: the mistake one makes in thinking that facts from different logical categories belong to the same category. Such a mistake would be made by someone who, after being shown all colleges, libraries, playing fields, scientific departments and administrative offices of

Oxford University, would insist that they have not seen the university. **Ryle** argues that **Cartesian** substance **dualism** makes the same mistake of positing a spurious extra member.

Causal Closure of the Physical: the principle, adhered to in scientific explanation, that every event has a physical cause, that the physical world is 'closed under causation'.

Causal Exclusion Principle: the principle, formulated by **Kim** and evidently supported by scientific practice, that no event can have two independent causes.

Causal Inheritance Principle: the principle, formulated by **Kim**, that a higher-order property has no causal powers other than those of its physical realiser on any given occasion.

Causal Laws: although the correct understanding of causation is open to debate, one generally accepted principle is *causal uniformity*, the view that nature remains uniform through its past, present and future states and that its laws are causal laws: unfailingly obtainable regularities between similar events and their effects. **Fodor** argues that a proper understanding of causal laws favours **non-reductive physicalism**. Basic sciences operate with *strict laws*: when $p \rightarrow q$ (read as 'if p, then q') is a strict law, the satisfaction of its antecedent necessitates the satisfaction of its consequent. Laws of **special sciences**, including *psychological* or *intentional laws*, are not strict: they obtain only when certain *ceteris paribus* clauses are satisfied as well (they have the form 'if p, then q all else being equal'). This may lead to the view (present in **anomalous monism** and **counterfactual causation** theories) that **mental events** must be subsumed by basic physical laws. However, Fodor argues, science can also operate with *ceteris paribus laws*, uncovering nature's regularities at higher levels of description. And if one can formulate (non-strict) causal laws about individuals in virtue of their possessing some property, this property must be seen as *causally responsible* for bringing about certain outcomes. Falling under the laws of **folk psychology**, intentional **mental properties** can be true causes of behaviour. Non-strict laws differ from strict ones not because they have exceptions, but because they require mechanisms of implementation at a more basic level. For Fodor, intentional laws have computational mechanisms of implementation, which is another reason to doubt their reducibility and the existence of **psychophysical laws**.

Further reading: Fodor (1989)

Causal Theory of Content see **Informational Theory of Content**

Causal Theory of Mind (causal role materialism): a species of the **identity theory** developed independently in the 1960s by David **Armstrong**, Brian Medlin and David **Lewis**. It stresses the role of the notion of causality in the explanation of **mental states**: a mental state is a state that is caused by certain external stimuli or other mental states and that, together with other mental states, causes behaviour. The causal role played by mental states allows for their identification with **brain** states, and the exact nature of identities must be established by empirical science.

Causal Theory of Reference (meaning): the view originated by **Kripke** that (at least some) words refer *directly* to objects in virtue of a causal relation that holds between them. Opposing **Frege's** distinction between **sense and reference** and **Russell's** theory of definite descriptions, Kripke

argued that the meaning of a proper name is its reference (anticipated by J. S. **Mill**). If one considers modal
contexts, one can see that proper names and coreferential with them definite descriptions do not have the same
meaning: although in our world Aristotle was the teacher
of Alexander the Great, in a different historical scenario
he might not have taught Alexander, but he would have
remained the same individual (the *modal argument*). Besides, we learn that Aristotle was the teacher of Alexander
from studying history, but this **knowledge** would have
to be a priori if the name and the description had the
same meaning (the *epistemological argument*), and people manage to refer to the same individuals even if they
know little about them or associate with them different
descriptions (the *transcendental* or *semantic argument*).
Distinguishing between contingent or **accidental properties** of individuals and their **essential properties**, Kripke
argued that names are *rigid designators* (they pick out the
same individuals in all **possible worlds**). A name becomes
attached to an individual in an act of *linguistic baptism*
and knowledge of its reference spreads among speakers
down a causal chain. The view was extended by Kripke
and **Putnam** (**Twin Earth, essentialism**) to **natural kind**
terms, leading to the emergence of **externalism** and the
informational theory of content.

Further reading: Kripke (1980)

Central State Materialism see **Armstrong, David M.**

Ceteris Paribus **Laws** see **Causal Laws**

Character see **Personality**

Chauvinism: any approach to the **mind** which entails that
only humans have certain mental features may be accused

of chauvinism. But its opposite, *liberalism*, may be accused of assigning mental characteristics too freely.

Cheater Detection Module see **Wason Selection Task**

Chinese Room: John **Searle**'s argument against strong **artificial intelligence**, **functionalism** and the **computational theory of mind**. Taking as an example Roger Schank's program which simulated human understanding of stories by producing correct answers to questions within a given scenario (for example, concluding that a man who was served a burned hamburger in a restaurant and left without paying had not eaten it), Searle argues that thinking cannot be **computation** because computer programs are not capable of understanding. Programs have only syntactic properties (they manipulate formal symbols), whereas **minds** also have **content** or **semantics**. Thus Searle imagines himself locked in a room with a lot of Chinese symbols and instructions in English which tell him what strings of symbols to hand back in response to what other strings of symbols that he is given through a window. He further imagines that he performs the task so well that he passes the **Turing test** for understanding Chinese, even though he has no knowledge of the language. In this **thought-experiment** Searle implements a program for understanding Chinese, but there is no understanding on his part. Hence, syntax is not sufficient for semantics. Critics reply that: (1) understanding is produced by a larger physical or virtual system of which Searle is only a part (situated at the level of the implementer, but not the implemented); (2) adding a robotic body with sensorimotor capacities or a detailed simulation of **brain** operations would endow the system with genuine understanding; (3) Searle confuses manipulating formal (unintepreted) symbols with performing formal operations on symbols (the issue of syntax is separate from that of semantics); (4) Searle speculates on our intuitions because we do not know how to define understanding in the case of systems different from ourselves in size and speed of processing.

Further reading: Searle (1980); Preston and Bishop (2002)

Chomsky, Noam A. (b.1928): American linguist, the initiator of the 'cognitive revolution'. Chomsky's poverty of stimulus argument and considerations regarding the productivity of language use led him to argue for the existence of the *language faculty*, a system of universal recursive rules of grammar innate in the human brain (*universal grammar*). Although Chomsky's syntactic theory has seen several changes since the 1960s (his recent minimalism postulates minimal representations and views the language acquisition device (LAD) as constrained by articulatory-perceptual and conceptual-intentional systems), his argumentation had a major impact on the resurrection of rationalism about cognitive capacities which can be viewed as part of our genetically determined biological endowment. Chomsky's views on linguistic competence as a body of innate domain-specific knowledge inaccessible to consciousness led to the development of psychological theories of tacit knowledge and gave rise to the notion of Chomskian modularity ('Chomskian modules' are not computational modules). But Chomsky is also sceptical of many problems in philosophy of mind: thus he thinks that intentionality cannot be part of a naturalistic inquiry into language and that the notion of broad content is meaningless because it plays no role in experimental theory construction. As he puts it, there are problems that can be solved by science and mysteries that cannot.

Further reading: Chomsky (2000)

Classical Theory of Concepts see **Definitional Theory**

Cognition: the way organisms acquire, store and use **knowledge** or **information**. Cognition encompasses **perception,** attention, object and pattern recognition, **memory, learning,** language processing, thinking, reasoning, planning, problem-solving and decision-making. The cognitive revolution of the mid-twentieth century was characterised by the increasing understanding that in their everyday behaviour organisms do not simply attend to immediate needs but try to find out about the world, to obtain information that may be relevant to future behaviour. Because organisms can only act out of what they represent and because the best known explanation of intelligent knowledge manipulation is computational, the notions of **representation** and **computation** are central to understanding the cognitive **mind.** However, the emphasis of classical **cognitive science** on the representational-computational explanation is questioned by those researchers who hold that it ignores our **embodiment,** our interaction with our physical and social environments (**embedded cognition**), the appetitive (bodily desires) and affective (**emotions**) sides of our mental life, and, finally, **consciousness.**

Cognitive: relating to **cognition.**

Cognitive Architecture: the **mind's/brain's** computational architecture, that is its internal organisation specified in terms of how it encodes and stores **information,** the operations it can carry out and the constraints (like limited **memory**) that govern its use of available resources. To explain how the mind works is to explain the relation between its architecture and the information it makes use of. That is, one must address the question of whether an observed regularity or behavioural pattern is due to the mind's internal organisation or to what is known by the organism. The two main accounts of cognitive architecture are the **computational theory of mind** and **connectionism** (sometimes **dynamical systems** theory is also added to them). The cognitive architecture debate is intertwined with debates about **innateness** versus **learning** (**rationalism** versus **empiricism**) and **modularity** versus domain-generality, but the issues involved are conceptually distinct and should not be confused.

Cognitive Closure: Colin McGinn's term for the view that there are problems which we (although, possibly, not beings with a radically different type of **mind**) will never be able to solve because we lack the ability to form adequate **concepts**. Thus a physicalistic explanation of (**phenomenal**) **consciousness** is cognitively closed for us because the scientific concepts we are capable of forming are inherently spatial in nature but our concepts of consciousness, formed via **introspection**, are not.

Further reading: McGinn (1989)

Cognitive Dissonance: absence of consistency in one's belief system. According to Leon Festinger who introduced the term (1957, *Theory of Cognitive Dissonance*) people tend to reduce dissonance by making suitable adjustments to their beliefs. Thus a person may rationalise their drink-driving by doubting the evidence about the disruptive effects of alcohol.

Cognitive Ethology: the study of **animal cognition** and behaviour originated by Donald Griffin who united **cognitive science** and ethology. Ethology was founded in the mid-1930s by Konrad Lorenz and Nico Tinbergen as an approach to animal behaviour which emphasised the need to study species-specific behaviour in natural settings. Lorenz introduced the notions of *imprinting* (the process by which chicks of some bird species become socially attached to their mothers) and *critical period*. He also argued that organisms' capacity for **learning** increases with the increase in the number of **innate** structures and characterised innate traits as products of genetic **information**. In the 1970s Griffin argued that the notions of **intentionality** and **consciousness** can be productively employed in animal research and his arguments were later taken up by a number of researchers. Although some theorists oppose the ascription of **mental states** to animals, such opposition often has an a priori character or is motivated by general mistrust of **mental concepts**. (**Dennett** is a major critic of cognitive ethology.) For philosophers who accept mental **realism** empirical data collected by cognitive ethologists can be used towards developing new approaches to problems in **philosophy of mind**.

Further reading: Allen and Bekoff (1997)

Cognitive Meaning see **Frege, Gottlob**

Cognitive Psychology: a branch of psychology studying **cognition** in controlled laboratory experiments. In the 1960s cognitive psychology replaced **methodological behaviourism** by requiring psychological explanation to be given in terms of internal structures and processes.

Cognitive Science: an interdisciplinary study of **mind** and **cognition** which emerged in the 1970s conjoining **cognitive psychology**, linguistics, **artificial intelligence**, philosophy and **logic**. Cognitive science is sometimes contrasted with **neuroscience** as a study of mind in abstraction from its realisation in the **brain**. But a better characterisation of their relationship is found in the *three-level (trilevel) hypothesis*, originated by **Marr**, according to which complex **information**-processing systems can be described at three different levels giving rise to distinct generalisations: the level of what the system does (its computational task, the **knowledge** or semantic level), the level of algorithms or procedures the system uses (the symbolic or syntactic level), and the level of physical or biological implementation of these procedures. The first two levels require the notions of **representation** and **computation**. Classical cognitive science thus combines the **representational** and **computational theory of mind**, but is challenged by other theories of **cognitive architecture**.

Further reading: Smith and Osherson (1995); Bechtel and Graham (1998)

Colour: the most discussed secondary quality. We automatically attribute colours to objects in visual **perception**, but what is their nature, how do we perceive them and what is the nature of *mental colours*, the qualitative properties of our colour experiences (*qualia*)? *Subjectivism* holds that colours are **mental properties** and do not exist in the physical world. It is motivated by the view that similarity relations between colours are their **essential properties** (Paul Boghossian and David Velleman). Subjectivism characterises the **sense-datum theory**, **adverbialism** and *projectivism* (the view that in perception mental colours are projected onto mind-independent objects, which has the consequence that colour experience is massively illusory). An influential approach was proposed by C. L. Hardin who identifies colours with neural events in the visual system (on the basis of such evidence as genetic abnormalities in colour vision). *Dispositionalism*, resisting a lack of contribution from the world, holds that colours are **dispositions** of physical objects to produce certain perceptual states. These have ineliminable colour *qualia* because the **what-it's-like** character of colours constitutes their essential property (John McDowell, Christopher Peacocke). **Physicalism** or colour **realism**, rejected by seventeenth-century science and resurrected by the **identity theory**, holds that colours are properties of physical objects, namely surface reflectances (**Armstrong, Smart**). David Hilbert shows that the constancy of perceived colours correlates with surface reflectance, which suggests that colour vision's biological function is the detection of physical objects by surface reflectances. A complication arises because of metamers, physical objects with different surface reflectances perceived as the same colour. This requires relativising to the visual system which is done differently by **representationalism about consciousness** and the ecological theory of Evan Thompson. Some physicalists also accept the existence of mental colours (David **Lewis**, Sydney Shoemaker).

Further reading: Hardin (1993); Thompson (1995)

Common-sense Functionalism see **Analytic Functionalism**

Compositionality: the property of thought in virtue of which the meaning or **content** of a complex **representation** is determined by the meanings of its constituents and the rules of their combination. Thus the meaning of GREEN TRIANGLE is determined by the meanings of GREEN and TRIANGLE, and TRIANGLE makes the same semantic contribution to GREEN TRIANGLE and RED TRIANGLE. Arguably, thought is productive and systematic because of its compositional structure, and compositionality is thus a major constraint on theories of **concepts**. As natural languages are not sufficiently compositional (they contain expressions like 'topless bar' or 'kick the bucket'), one needs to posit a **language of thought** where compositionality is not violated.

Computation: rule-governed or algorithmic transition between states of a system which has the function of organising and manipulating **information** available to the system. In this sense, speaking of **mind** as a computer is not metaphorical. In fact, the word 'computer' was used by **Turing** (and well before him) to designate a person doing calculation. One of the reasons for using the notion of computation as given by the **computational theory of mind** is that one needs a level of explanation where thought processes can be depicted as **content**-sensitive and truth-preserving. And it is not clear if one can explain these properties of thought at the neural level, especially if one accepts the **multiple realisability** thesis (viewing the mind as 'the software of the **brain**'). However, it is also possible to speak of computation in the **brain**, and a model exploiting this possibility is proposed by **connectionism**. Yet the notion of computation itself was criticised by **Searle** as unscientific because, unlike intrinsic features of the world studied by fundamental sciences, computation is observer-relative: state transitions are computations only if somebody interprets them as such. Thus nothing can be a computer by itself ('syntax is not intrinsic to physics') and the question whether the mind/brain is one lacks sense. This criticism is, however, invalidated if one concedes that computations are state transitions governed by counterfactual supporting, hence interpretation-independent, rules. The notion of computation as inside-the-skull process is questioned by **dynamical systems** and **extended mind** theories (sometimes called post-computational approaches).

Computational Theory of Mind (CTM, classical CTM, symbolicism): the view that the **mind** is an **information**-processing system and that **cognitive** mental processes (thinking, perceiving) can be understood in terms of **computation**. CTM became prominent in the 1980s consolidating the insights of **Turing**, **von Neumann**, **Putnam** and **Fodor**. It holds that mental processes are computational-inferential operations carried on syntactically structured mental **representations**. Being symbols in the **language of thought**, representations have both **content** and material (formal, syntactic) properties to which computational mechanisms are sensitive. The notion of syntactic encoding explains how a physical system can have semantic properties and how mental processes can be causal physical processes. The similarity between our **cognitive architecture** and the architecture of the digital computer consists in symbolic code manipulation: mental symbols are discrete content-bearing entities which are manipulated in accordance with structure-sensitive rules hard-wired into the mind/**brain**. However, CTM faces several challenges and objections. One challenge came from recognising that many **intentional states** (beliefs, desires) have **broad content** which does not seem relevant to scientific psychology. Reactions to this still much-discussed issue include viewing the mind as a **syntactic engine**, isolating **narrow content** (**internalism**) and arguing for the relevance of broad content (**externalism**). Objections to CTM include its formal character and the seeming disregard of content (**Chinese room, symbol grounding problem**), its insensitivity to biological details and statistical factors (**connectionism**), and its inability to explain the global character of thought processes (**abduction, frame problem**).

Further reading: Pylyshyn (1984); Block (1995b)

Conceivability Arguments: arguments like that from **zombies** which build on the intuition that if something is conceivable, it is metaphysically possible.

Concept Acquisition see **Learning**

Concepts: constituents of thought expressed by individual words (more precisely, morphemes) and phrases.

Someone who can think that cats eat fish must have the concepts CAT, EAT and FISH. Small capital letters are the accepted notation used to distinguish concepts from words and discussions centre on (1) concepts expressed by predicates ('is a cat'), (2) *lexical* concepts expressed by simple morphemes and corresponding to a language's lexicalised vocabulary. Many issues about concepts are part of the larger issue of **content** and **intentionality**, but the problem is also addressed in **cognitive psychology** and the questions of what concepts are and what it is to possess a concept are answered differently by the older **image theory** and **definitional theory** and the more recent **functional role semantics, prototype theory, exemplar theory, theory theory** and **informational atomism**. Arguably, a theory of concepts must explain concept robustness (stability of content), **compositionality** and shareability (in order to communicate different people must have the same concepts). However, according to **Fodor**, only informational atomism meets these constraints. Thus most theories connect having concepts with having **knowledge** or epistemic capacities: someone who has the concept CAT knows how to tell cats from noncats, what judgements are true of cats, what typical cats look like and what other features they have. Psychologists sometimes talk about *conceptual change* which is characteristic of children's acquisition of adult-like concepts (conceptions) and adults' scientific development. But what knowledge or beliefs are constitutive of concept possession? If this view leads to **holism**, the connection between psychology and **epistemology** may seem less convincing.

Further reading: Margolis and Laurence (1999); Murphy (2002)

Conceptual Role Semantics see **Functional Role Semantics**

Connectionism: a computational approach to the **mind/brain**
which opposes the classical **computational theory of mind**
on the issues of **cognitive architecture** and mental **representation**. Connectionist models are *artificial neural networks (nets)* consisting of layers of interconnected units
resembling **neurons**. For modelling such tasks as face
recognition the modeller specifes what microfeatures are
detected by 'sensory' input units assigned different activation values. Input units activate 'internal processing'
hidden units, which then activate output units. All units
are linked via excitatory or inhibitory connections assigned different *weights*, and the activation values of
'non-sensory' units depend on the activation values of
units inputing to them and connection weights (reflecting
statistical regularities of feature correlation in the environment). Except in 'localist models', individual internal
processing units do not have determinate semantic properties. That is, because networks have no internal structure, there are no discrete representations of properties
(no symbols like NOSE) and no separately stored representations of transformational rules, but all representations
are distributed over multiple units and stored implicitly
in connection patterns. All **contents**, represented as *activation vectors* in a multidimensional space, belong to the
system's global state and all transformational processes
occur in parallel (hence *parallel distributed processing
or PDP*). The system learns to process inputs correctly
through *backpropagation* (small adjustments of connection weights by the modeller). First developed in the
1950s, connectionist models (run on digital computers)
became prominent in the 1980s. But although PDP can account for statistically sensitive **learning**, it cannot explain
structure-sensitive **thought and language** processing because it has no resources to model their **systematicity** (see
associationism). This led some researchers to hold that

the mind contains different kinds of representations or explore connectionism's potential for modelling the *implementation* of classical architecture in the brain, whereas other attempt to overthrow the systematicity argument.

Further reading: Rumelhart and McClelland (1986)

Consciousness: that aspect of **mind** which necessarily involves reference to how things are for the subject; subjective awareness or experience. This, however, admits of different readings and explains the multiplicity of notions current in the literature. Philosophers are mostly interested in **phenomenal consciousness,** the qualitative character of experience (*qualia,* **what-it's-like**). It is possible to distinguish from it **access consciousness** and, further, *reflexive* or *monitoring consciousness,* which is consciousness of being in a certain **mental state.** The awareness of oneself as the subject of experience is **self-consciousness,** and one's overall conscious state is referred to as the **unity of consciousness.** Another two important distinctions are (1) that between *creature consciousness* and *state consciousness* (should one define conscious creatures in terms of conscious states or the other way round?) and (2) that between the *transitive* (consciousness *of*) and *intransitive* notions of consciousness. The crucial questions are: why does the relevant sort of consciousness exist? how does it change, if at all, the mental lives of creatures who have it? what sort of creatures have it? what difference does it make to mental states and processes?

Further reading: Rosenthal (1986); Smith and Jokic (2003)

Consciousness, Scientific Explanations of: can be subdivided into **cognitive** and neurological. Cognitive theories try to give a functional characterisation of **consciousness.** Thus in Bernard Baars' Global Workspace theory, the **brain** contains many specialised modules which process

information at a subconscious level, but when it is useful for several modules to have access to some information it becomes 'broadcast' across the cognitive system in the form of conscious **mental states** so that their **content** can be used in more flexible ways. Neurological theories aim to differentiate between kinds or states of consciousness (like minimal consciousness) and establish their neural correlates (NCCs). To date, the best electrophysiological correlate of **phenomenal consciousness** is the coherent 40 Hz gamma oscillation generated by the brain. According to Francis Crick and Christof Koch, it is produced by synchronous firing of thalamo-cortical **neurons** representing different bits of sensory information, which also suggests a solution to the **binding problem**. This view is questioned by some researchers who argue that the synchrony cannot be maintained by synaptic mechanisms (**quantum theories of consciousness**). Questions for philosophical reflection include: (1) since correlation is not identity, can NCCs explain the hard problem and close the **explanatory gap**? and (2) given that much research concerns the correlates of phenomenal awareness in different sensory modalities (particularly **vision**), can one speak of (phenomenal) consciousness as a single property constituting a **natural kind**?

Further reading: Baars (1988); Koch (2004)

Consciousness, Theories of: few philosophers today endorse substance **dualism** about the **self** (but see **person**), and many contemporary approaches may be labelled *cognitivism*: they attempt to understand **consciousness** as a **cognitive** phenomenon, in terms of **intentionality** and **representation** (**higher-order theories**, **Dennett**, Paul and Patricia Churchland). The main principle behind this research, anticipated by **Hume**, can be stated as 'no consciousness without **content**'. **Representationalism about consciousness** and the **phenomenal concepts**

approach use it to explain **phenomenal consciousness**. This trend is opposed by philosophers who argue for dualism about *qualia* and the **what-it's-like** character of experience (early **Jackson**, David Chalmers and Thomas Nagel, who used to think that **physicalism** about consciousness is possible if one develops **concepts** that make the first- and third-person perspectives logically inseparable). It is also opposed by philosophers who think that the phenomenal character of **mental states** cannot be explained by their representational content (Ned Block, Christopher Peacocke), that there is close connection between consciousness and intentionality, that the phenomenal intentionality of experience has explanatory priority (Colin McGinn, Charles Siewert, Terence Horgan and John Tienson), and that intentionality must itself be explained in terms of consciousness (**phenomenology**, **Searle**, Galen Strawson).

Further reading: McGinn (1991); Siewert (1998); Horgan and Tienson (2002)

Constructivism: the view that reality is socially or culturally constructed. Constructivism about **colour** holds that colour is a culturally constructed property so that to be red is to satisfy cultural criteria for the application of the predicate 'red' (J. Van Brakel). Constructivism about **emotions** understands them as learnt behaviours reflecting social norms (Rom Harré).

Content: that which a mental **representation** (**concept**, thought, subpersonal state) represents or is about. Thus the content of the state of believing that it is cold is the proposition that it is cold (at the place where the person having this belief is). One problem in the discussion of **intentionality** is the ascription of contentful **intentional states**. But even if one agrees with **folk psychology** that states with determinate contents can be ascribed to individuals, there are more problems to solve. Do representations have contents in virtue of their causal connections with the world (**informational theory of content**), their functional role within an organism (**teleological theory of content**) or their role in reasoning (**functional role semantics**)? Do individuals' concepts and thoughts essentially depend on their environment (**externalism**) and have **broad content** (intentional or referential content; Russellian content, if one thinks, after early **Russell**, that contentful states involve real-world objects and properties)? Or do they only depend on how things appear to individuals (**internalism**) and have **narrow content** (Fregean or **cognitive** content for it involves **Frege's** senses or **modes of presentation**)? Or is their content broad but Fregean? And what can one say about **perception** (**phenomenal** states generally)? Perceptual experience allows us to form beliefs about the world, but is its representational content *conceptual* or *propositional* like that of belief? We probably see more than we can conceptualise: does it follow that perception involves **non-conceptual content** or only a species of **demonstrative content**?

Contingent Property see **Accidental Property**

Counterfactual Causation: an approach to **mental causation** developed by Ernest Lepore and Barry Loewer to argue for **non-reductive physicalism**. It holds that although an event's causal powers are completely determined by its physical properties, **mental properties** qua mental are nonetheless *causally relevant* to the production of behaviour. Causality is understood here not in terms of **causal laws,** but in terms of counterfactuals ('If John had not thought there was beer in the fridge, he would not have gone to the kitchen') as analysed in **Lewis's possible**

worlds approach. Consider a mental event m which has both a physical property P and a mental property M and which causes a behavioural outcome b. It seems that P is necessary for the causation of b. But on the other hand, due to **multiple realisability** of mental properties, P as such is not necessary for the causation of b, because the counterfactual $-Pm \& Mm \rightarrow b$ is true: m would have caused b even if it did not have the physical property P but had instead the physical property P^*. **Kim** objects that this still leaves mental causation **epiphenomenal**, and to counteract this charge Loewer questions the notion of causation as production.

Further reading: Lepore and Loewer (1989)

Covariance Approaches to Content see **Informational Theory of Content**

Creativity: psychological capacity involving **productivity, imagination,** inventiveness, originality, impredictability and a sense of aesthetic quality. Because outcome of computers seems to be predictable, creativity poses a major challenge to **artificial intelligence** research (why do most people decline to consider short stories composed by computers as products of creative processes?).

Further reading: Boden (2003)

Davidson, Donald (1917–2003): American philosopher, the originator of **anomalous monism**. In his philosophy of language, Davidson employs the notion of truth definition developed by Alfred Tarski (1901–83) for analysing truth in formalised languages (for example, 'Snow is white' is true iff snow is white; convention T). But whereas Tarski's analysis is neutral on the issue of mental **representation,**

Davidson, in his defence of **radical interpretation,** takes the notion of truth rather than that of translation for granted. Observing what sentences speakers of a language judge as true, the interpreter can come up with a theory of meaning for that language. For Davidson, meaning is reference, and in assigning referents to words the interpreter relies on the **principle of charity** maximising speakers' **rationality.** Davidson also holds that thought emerges together with natural language. Language learners learn to associate sentences with situations, and the context of **learning** itself favours **externalism.** They also learn to use words correctly, which makes meaning depend on the causal history of judgements (causal theory of meaning). However, Davidson opposes the **causal theory of reference** (understanding reference in causal terms) because of the dependence of reference on truth, the **indeterminacy of translation** and the **inscrutability of reference.** His view that **intentional states** are not real entities but rather modifications of persons makes him a proponent of **interpretivism** and **adverbialism.**

Further reading: Davidson (1984)

de dicto see *de re* **versus** *de dicto*

de re versus *de dicto*: the distinction between two different ways of interpreting sentences made clear by **Russell's** ('On Denoting') example about a touchy yacht owner to whom a guest remarked 'I thought your yacht was larger than it is', and who replied 'No, my yacht is not larger than it is'. The owner's reply is *de re*, about a particular thing, whereas the guest's remark is *de dicto*, about the idea he had formed of the yacht.

de se: *de se* thoughts are thoughts about oneself (thoughts with egocentric **content**) expressed with the help of the **indexical** 'I'. According to John Perry and David Kaplan, to entertain self-conscious thoughts is to have mastered the use of the first-person pronoun, and the **cognitive** role of 'I' is its character ('the thinker of the thought'). The difficulty with *de se* reports is that they cannot be analysed as *de re* or *de dicto*, because people may be unaware of themselves under some particular name or description (like people with amnesia, severe **memory** loss). Gareth Evans argued that **self-consciousness** is at the heart of the problem and thinking of oneself as oneself does not depend on being able to exploit public linguistic devices. Gabriel Segal further notes that people with **autism**, incapable of representing themselves as thinkers, do not lack the capacity to think of themselves. Because many of our thoughts are *de se* (all indexical and tensed thoughts like 'It's raining' seem to presuppose self-perspectivalness), **Lewis** holds that this counts in favour of **internalism**.

Further reading: Evans (1982)

Deference see **Broad Content**

Definitional theory (classical theory): identifies **concepts** with individually necessary and jointly sufficient conditions of their satisfaction known to competent users of them. The theory was outlined by **Plato** and later became associated with **Russell**'s and Moore's conceptual analysis (determination of the logical structure of concepts), reaching its peak in **logical positivism**. The theory proved untenable because definitions cannot exhaustively give the **content** of most concepts, and people do not know the definitions of such common concepts as SNOW, BEAUTIFUL or GAME. Problems arise even for 'a bachelor is an unmarried man' because one would not think of a catholic priest as a bachelor. The theory's failure had to do with its attempt to analyse concepts in terms of their ultimate constituents (**empiricism**) and identify concept possession with **knowledge** of definitions (**verificationism**). However, it contains an important idea that there must be some conditions which account for the content of concepts, and its impact is felt in subsequent approaches and lexical semantics ('the Neoclassical theory').

Deflationism: to be a deflationist about X is to downplay (allegedly) its significance by analysing it in terms of something else. Deflationism about (**phenomenal**) **consciousness** is the view that it can be a priori analysed in non-phenomenal terms of function or **representation** thus allowing for its **reduction** (the opposite of deflationism is 'inflationism').

Delusions: persistent false beliefs characteristic of **schizophrenia**.

Demonstrative Content: thought **content** specifiable with the help of pure ('this', 'that') or complex demonstratives ('this book', 'that man'). Because such thoughts are object-dependent, they pose a problem for **internalism** (although they may also have **narrow content** because one can use demonstratives to pick out different objects or even fail to pick out anything as in the case of **hallucination**). Demonstrative thought plays an especially prominent role in the *strong* **externalism** of Gareth Evans and John McDowell which holds that demonstrative **modes of presentation** constitutively depend on the objects they pick out so that your thought about a pen you see in front of you would be different in **content** were it an identical-looking but a different pen. (This position is thus different from 'mild externalism' in that it accepts **Frege**'s senses, even though it views them as *de re* senses.) McDowell also argues that perceptual content involves irreducible demonstrative **concepts** rather than **non-conceptual content**.

Dennett, Daniel C. (b.1942): American philosopher, a critic of the problems of **intentionality** and **consciousness**. Dennett holds that intentionality is not an intrinsic property of **mental states** but a construct arising from the **intentional stance** towards systems' behaviour. While this may be seen as 'mild **realism**', his views on consciousness are closer to **eliminativism**. He discards the *Cartesian theatre* model of consciousness where experiences as raw 'givens' pass before the internal observer, the conscious **self**. Instead he offers the Multiple Drafts Model where consciousness emerges from interacting **cognitive** capacities. Like health, consciousness is not a simple property of organisms. (Dennett's **homuncular functionalism** draws similar conclusions about intentionality.) There is no threshold separating the preconscious from consciousness, no special place where 'it all comes together', but at various times different **contents** acquire prominence in the cognitive system ('cerebral celebrity') and become manifest in verbal reports. However, Dennett does not dismiss **introspection** as completely misleading, holding that introspective reports are just another form of evidence that has no privileged status over psychophysical or neurological evidence (hence *heterophenomenology* – **phenomenology** from another's point of view). Our illusion of being conscious selves arises from the crucial role of internalised natural language in our kind of consciousness, where the narrative constructed by different subsystems helps control cognitive resources (language also creates for us the illusion of intentionality).

Further reading: Dennett (1991, 2005)

Depth Problem: an objection to the **causal theory of reference** and causal or informational accounts of **content** that one cannot say whether a type of mental **representation** represents *distal* objects (cats) rather than *proximal* stimuli (a certain type of retinal excitation). The best response is that proximal projections of a kind of object are so variable that a mechanism of **perception** which depended on them only would not succeed in detecting this kind of object at all.

Descartes, René Cartesius (1596–1650): French mathematician, the founder of **modern philosophy**. Given Descartes' prominent role in the emerging science, his philosophy is best understood from his aspiration towards a unified science resting on secure foundations of **knowledge** and his geometric conception of matter. The starting point is the *method of doubt* (Cartesian doubt or Cartesian **scepticism**, although the latter term is misleading as to Descartes' project) which urges one to reject any proposition whose truth may be doubted. The evil demon (*le malin génie*) can deceive one about the physical world, but knowledge of one's current thoughts or experience is not so susceptible. *Cogito ergo sum* (I think, therefore I am) is that foundation which underlies our capacity to form clear and distinct **ideas** of things that contain no contradiction and give the reason access to truth. Arguably, Descartes' **dualism, rationalism** and **representationalism** all follow from this. And as it is possible to conceive of one's **mind** existing without one's body and surviving the annihilation of the physical world, the two must be distinct and independent entities: the mental substance (*res cogitans*), the **mind** or the conscious **self** whose **essential property** is thinking, and the extended substance (*res extensa*) which encompasses the spatial world.

Further reading: Descartes (1984–85)

Design Stance see **Intentional Stance**

Determinism: the view that every event has a determinate cause in the previously existing state of affairs. This, however, does not imply that the whole evolution of the world is predetermined or that nothing can be unpredictable in principle.

Direct Perception: the thesis, developed in opposition to **representationalism**, that **perception** (particularly **vision**) is not mediated by inferential processes operating on complex, hierarchically structured internal **representations**. Its most prominent modern version is found in James J. Gibson's (1904–79) *ecological approach*. Emphasising that vision must be understood in terms of organisms' active exploration of the world, Gibson argued that perception is a direct pickup of **information** afforded to organisms by the environment. Instead of understanding visual processing in computational terms, one can compare the mind to the resonator: sense organs are 'tuned' to respond to certain types of physical energy called *invariants*. Higher-order invariants, or stable combinations of visually detected properties, constitute environmental *affordances* relevant to the abilities of kinds of organisms: containing information about possibilities for **action** (like locating food sources or avoiding obstacles), they guide the behaviour of organisms directly without the need for internal **computation**. Similar ideas were developed more recently by Kevin O'Regan and Alva Noë in their *sensorimotor theory of vision*, according to which seeing is a way of acting, of 'probing' the environment which serves as its own representation. When an organism masters the relevant *sensorimotor contingencies* (a kind of **knowledge-how** or implicit **knowledge** of correlations between actions and resulting perceptions), it acquires the experience of seeing (thus, seeing a bottle is knowing implicitly how its appearance changes as one moves in relation to it; in this respect, seeing is similar to touching). Because there are no internal representations, the problem of *qualia* does not emerge (for example, the experience of seeing red arises from 'sampling' portions of the environment). However, the approach meets the same difficulties as **behaviourism** and cannot accommodate evidence from lesion studies such as the existence of visual agnosia (visual integration failure).

Further reading: Gibson (1979); O'Regan and Noë (2001)

Direct Realism: the view that we directly perceive external world objects. This may be understood in three ways: (1) as *naive realism*, the view that the external world is the way it is presented to us in experience; (2) as a **direct perception** thesis; (3) as the view that our awareness of the world is direct in the sense of not being consciously inferential. Whereas naive realism runs up against the possibility of **illusion** and the problem of secondary qualities, direct realism avoids these difficulties for it denies only that we are first aware of our **sense-data** or internal **representations** and then infer on their basis the existence of physical reality (as in the case of seeing things on a closed-circuit television screen). Evidently, we can become aware of the quality of our experiences themselves, but rather than refute direct realism, this raises the issue of how our direct awareness of the world is mediated by complex neurophysiological processes and representational states.

Direct Reference see **Causal Theory of Reference**

Direction of Fit see **Intentional States**

Disjunction Problem: arises for **naturalised semantics** approaches. A mental **representation** of type R (COW) may be caused by various sorts of things (cows or horses on a dark night). The problem is to explain why its **content** is something less than the disjunction of its possible causes, especially as disjunctive content would result in the maximal correlation between the representation and the environment where it functions.

Disjunctivism: a theory of **perception** which opposes **representationalism,** holding that it cannot account for the **mind**'s 'openness' to the world and emphasising that genuine perceiving is a relational state which has mind-independent objects or object – involving **Frege**'s senses as its constituents (J. M. Hinton, Paul Snowdon, John McDowell, M. G. F. Martin). Arguing that dependence on physical objects is essential to the nature of perception, its proponents deny that genuine perception and **illusion/hallucination** belong to the same psychological kind ('the common kind assumption'). Even though they may feel subjectively the same, a perceptual experience is *either* a genuine perception *or* a hallucination. However, while accepting the **direct perception** thesis for genuine experiences, disjunctivists are forced to adopt representationalism for non-veridical experiences to account for their intentional **content.** This raises doubts about the psychological distinctness of veridical and non-veridical perception, given that both can serve as the basis for belief and **action** because of their content.

Further reading: McDowell (1994); Martin (2004)

Dispositional: (1) a **mental state** is dispositional if it is not **occurrent**; (2) an analysis is dispositional if it is done in terms of **dispositions**.

Dispositions: capacities of things to manifest certain behaviour in specified conditions. Thus fragility and solubility can be viewed as dispositional properties: a substance is soluble if it dissolves when placed in water. The causal status of dispositions is subject to debate: although they are functional properties and scientific terms are functionally determined, dispositions must be grounded in things' intrinsic properties. (This is the problem of *virtus dormitiva* satirised by Molière: to say that opium puts people to sleep because of its it dormitive virtue is not to give a causal explanation.) The notion of dispositions was also employed in **logical behaviourism**, beginning with **Ryle's** analysis of **knowledge-how**. According to Ryle, ascriptions of beliefs or emotional states are hypothetical statements about a person's behaviour under certain conditions. However, this analysis is problematic: people's dispositions to behaviour themselves depend on what psychological states they are in. Thus people who know how to play chess may not always have the disposition to move chess pieces in the way that is thought to be constitutive of their competence: their dispostions are different if they are playing with a child to whom they wish to lose a game. However, the dispositional analysis of beliefs still appears attractive to philosophers who think that beliefs cannot be stored in the **brain**. If beliefs are individuated by their truth-conditions, then saying that they are represented seems to commit one to the view that people are logically omniscient, which they are not (**entailment, KK-thesis**).

Further reading: Armstrong et al. (1996)

Distributed Representation see **Representation**

Doxastic: relating to belief. To represent a **content** doxastically is to represent it in belief.

Dreaming: the state of having experiences similar to perceptions which occurs during rapid eye movement (REM) sleep to most people. Closely emulating our wakeful experience (rich visual **phenomenology**, the egocentric perspective, felt **emotions**, formation of beliefs about what is happening), it raises questions about the nature of perception, imagery and (phenomenal) consciousness (the existence of *qualia*).

Dretske, Fred (b.1932): American philosopher, one of the originators of the **informational theory of content, externalism** and **representationalism about consciousness**. In his later work, Dretske distinguishes between indication and **representation**. Indication has to do with **information**-carrying, is widespread and sufficient for minimal **intentionality**. Representation, however, requires the notion of function (paper clips can carry information about temperature, but they cannot misrepresent it, because that is not their job). Thus the informational approach must be combined with the **teleological theory of content** to give mental states their functions. Natural selection gives **content** to perceptual or **phenomenal** states, and **learning** to conceptual states (states, like beliefs, for being in which one needs to have **concepts**). Dretske's solution to the **disjunction problem**, however, appeals not to teleology, but to the theses that information is relative to circumstances and that truly mental representation can arise only in systems capable of the right kind of learning.

Further reading: Dretske (1981, 2000)

Dual-Aspect Semantics see **Two-Factor Theories**

Dual-Aspect Theory see **Dualism**

Dualism: the view that the mental and the physical constitute two different realms of reality. *Substance dualism* is the view, associated with **Descartes**, that **minds** and bodies belong to completely distinct kinds – the immaterial thinking substance and the material extended substance which, nonetheless, can enter into causal interactions (Cartesian **interactionism**). *Attribute dualism* (*double-* or *dual-aspect theory*) is the view, associated with **Spinoza**, that whereas there is only one substance, the mental and the physical are different, independent kinds of properties: although they can be instantiated in the same objects, **mental properties** cannot be identified with physical properties. Attribute dualism is sometimes called *property dualism*, but one must be careful with the latter term because it is sometimes applied to **non-reductive physicalism** which also holds that mental and physical properties are distinct kinds of properties but, unlike dual-aspect theories, accepts the dependence of the mental on the physical. A prominent contemporary double-aspect theory is found in David Chalmers' theory of **phenomenal consciousness** which views conscious properties as basic constituents of reality on a par with fundamental physical properties. According to it, **information** is embodied both in the physical-functional and the phenomenal information spaces, which stand in direct isomorphism to one another. There is only one abstract information space but it has two distinct aspects. The ubiquitousness of information brings this theory close to **panpsychism** and Chalmers himself refers to it as *panprotopsychism*.

Further reading: Chalmers (1996)

Dynamical Systems (dynamicism): an approach to **cognition** which views cognitive agents as dynamical systems. Dynamical systems theory is mathematical modelling of the behaviour of complex systems (like the meteorological system of our planet) using non-linear differential equations. Dynamical systems are open: variables and parameters determining the system's development in time are not wholly internal to it (thus in modelling the meteorological system one must keep track of the Sun's energy arriving at different locations). They are open-ended: their development from an initial point can follow distinct trajectories. They are continuously changing, deterministic, and involve no internal **information** use by their components.

Several researchers (Timothy van Gelder, Robert Port, Rodney Brooks, Esther Thelen, Linda B. Smith) argue today that dynamicism can supplant the **computational theory of mind** and **connectionism** (which also employs the notions of **computation** and **representation**). Its main ideas are **embedded cognition** and 'intelligence without representation': organisms and their environments are parts of the same dynamical system; changes in the system are not mediated by discrete information-carrying states internal to organisms; cognitive agents are constituted by many interacting dynamical systems (horizontal instead of vertical **modularity**); cognition emerges from cycles of **perception–action**–perception. Dynamical systems approach was used to model locomotion (Scott Kelso) and insect navigation (Brooks; situated robotics). However, despite common disclaimers, dynamical systems modelling does not eliminate computation (all simulations are run on digital computers) and representation (variables are assigned discrete quantities, and state-transitions are rule-governed). Rather, what dynamisists about cognition deny is that rules and **contents** are explicitly represented in the **minds** of agents. However, although this may be true of some processes, it poses the same question that baffled **behaviourism**: what kind of behaviour is thinking?

Further reading: Brooks (1991); van Gelder (1998)

Ecological Perception see **Direct Perception**

Egocentric Content see *de se*

Eliminative Materialism: the view that our common-sense understanding of people's behaviour in terms of their **mental states** and the corresponding **mental concepts** should be eliminated from scientific psychology. Eliminative materialism arose in the 1970s from dissatisfaction with **Nagelian reduction** and acceptance of **Quine**'s views on the impossibility of **intentional** science (Paul Feyerabend, Richard Rorty and Paul Churchland). In his attack on **folk psychology** Churchland argued that it has all the features of a false scientific theory, that the entities it postulates are similar in nature to phlogiston or alchemical essences and will have to be discarded by future science. Replacing folk psychology, **neuroscience** will show that there is nothing like beliefs and desires in the **brain**. The same fate awaits folk ideas of **consciousness**, *qualia* and the **self**, and this aspect of **eliminativism** was especially welcomed by **Dennett**. However, it is not obvious that mental concepts are theoretical constructs rather than part of our psychological make-up (**theory of mind**). More recent developments of eliminative materialism moved away from the issue of the scientific status of folk psychology and continue to exist under the name of **neurophilosophy**.

Further reading: Churchland (1981); Churchland and Churchland (1998)

Eliminativism: to be an eliminativist about *X* is to hold that *X* is merely a word of everyday language for which there is no corresponding reality and it thus has to be eliminated from scientific explanation (see **eliminative materialism**).

Embedded Cognition: the term for theories that oppose the **computational** and **representational theory of mind** by emphasising that it ignores the fact that **cognition** is embedded in the **brain** (**connectionism**) and in the body (**embodiment**), and is situated in the world (**dynamical systems, extended mind, direct perception**), being essentially enactive (**action**). Instead of 'detached', input–output, centrally mediated processes, they propose that spatially situated body–environment interactions are constitutive of **intelligence**, and that **rationality** consists in adaptive responses.

Embodiment: the fact that we are not pure **minds** but minds embedded in bodies. The thesis that organisms' **cognition** is shaped by their gross bodily form allows for readings of different strength. Thus Dana Ballard argued that orienting movements may constrain the way **information** about objects is processed at a less abstract level than that of symbolic reasoning (local problem-solving mechanisms). The more radical views are that **concepts** emerge from embodied schemas (George Lakoff, Mark Johnson) or that intelligent **action** does not require representation (**dynamical systems, extended mind, direct perception, Merleau-Ponty**).
Further reading: Ballard et al. (1997)

Emergentism: the view that properties of complex systems are *emergent* from the properties of their constituents, being unpredictable from and irreducible to their combinations. Emergentism was espoused by several British philosophers and scientists in the early twentieth century (C. Lloyd Morgan, Samuel Alexander, C. D. Broad) as a position concerning the status of chemical and biological properties. (The idea that products of chemical reactions are emergent properties traces to J. S. **Mill**, although it was abandoned in the twentieth century with the availability of the quantum mechanical explanation of chemical bonding, leading to the demise of emergentism.) **Mind** or **consciousness** (the terms were used interchangeably) was similarly understood as an emergent property of the **brain**. Central to emergentism is the 'many-layers' view of reality: each level of increasing complexity (the biological level above the chemical level, the conscious mental level above the biological level) has its own novel causal properties irreducible to those of a certain constellation of lower-level properties. Note that emergentism viewed **reduction** as an explanatory rather than ontological issue: consciousness is emergent and irreducible because we cannot explain why a certain level of complexity of physiological organisation should possess it. This distinguishes emergentism from many versions of contemporary **nonreductive physicalism**, although both approaches face the problem of accounting for the irreducibility of the mental without violating the **causal closure of the physical.**

Further reading: Broad [1925] (1976)

Emotions: such **phenomenal** states as admiration, anger, annoyance, anxiety, awe, benevolence, compassion, contrition, disgust, distress, embarrassment, empathy, ennui, envy, euphoria, fear, grief, gratitude, guilt, happiness, hate, hope, humility, indignation, jealousy, joy, love, nostalgia, pride, rage, regret, remorse, resentment, sadness, shame, sorrow, sympathy, surprise, worry, wrath. Only six emotions are considered as basic and accompanied by universally recognisable facial expressions: happiness, surprise, sadness, anger, disgust and fear, and they may constitute **natural kinds.** But is 'emotion' a natural kind term? What is the relation between emotions and bodily feelings (**sensations**) and disturbances (blushing, perspiring)? The accepted view today is that emotions are object-directed (emotional **intentionality**), which distinguishes them from **moods,** but some emotions, like sadness, may be an exception to that. The relation between emotions (**passions**) and **rationality** is also an important issue. Emotions are involuntary in character – they simply happen to us – but we also think of them as inappropriate or inadequate to the behaviour of a rational agent in particular situations. Neuroscientist Antonio Damasio argues that emotions are crucial to decision-making, serving as 'somatic markers' in the **brain**'s function of monitoring the organism's past and future responses (damage to prefrontal and somatosensory areas leads to diminished emotion and impaired practical **intelligence**). Emotions also seem involved in maintaining adequate belief formation (**schizophrenia**) and regulating social relations (moral emotions or emotions of **self-consciousness**).

Further reading: Damasio (1999)

Emotions, Theories of: the first psychological theory of **emotions,** the James-Lange theory, was proposed by William **James** (1884) and Dutch psychologist Carl G. Lange (1885). The theory identifies emotions with bodily feelings (**sensations**) and physiological disturbances: we feel sadness because we cry and fear because we tremble. In the late 1920s it was replaced by the Cannon-Bard theory (Walter Cannon, Philip Bard) which views emotions as independent of physiological change detection: identical physiological changes accompany different emotions (fear and anger) and non-emotional states (fever). Since the 1960s the leading philosophical theory of emotions has been the **cognitive** theory which identifies emotions with evaluative judgements and analyses them in terms of **intentional states** like beliefs and desires. Thus fear of a snake is constituted by the belief that it might bite and the desire not to be bitten. According to its strong versions (Robert Solomon, Richard Lazarus), emotions are just rational appraisals, not irrational drives. According to the mild versions or hybrid theories (William Lycan, Martha Nussbaum) they also have crucial affective components. But the cognitive theory apparently cannot explain the divergence between emotion and belief (believing that flying is safe does not eliminate the fear), emotions' **phenomenal** feel and the fact that propositional **contents** associated with emotions can occur without them. Alternative approaches are offered by the affect program theory (Paul Ekman, Paul Griffiths, Craig DeLancey; pioneered by Charles Darwin) which views emotions as complex adaptive responses and addresses only the basic emotions, and **evolutionary psychology** which explores the idea of the **modularity** of other emotions as well.

Further reading: Lewis and Haviland-Jones (2000)

Empirical Functionalism see **Machine Functionalism**

Empiricism: the view that all **knowledge** is based on sensory experience, that there is nothing in the **mind** that was not first in the senses (*nihil in intellectu nisi prius in sensu*). British empiricists **Locke** and **Hume** held that at birth the **mind** is a blank slate (*tabula rasa*), that **ideas** are copies from sensory states or combinations of such copies (**image theory**), and that thoughts are associations of ideas (**associationism**). In response **Leibniz** and **Kant** argued that the mind must contain **innate** categories with which to organise sensory experience. **Concept** empiricism was recently revived by researchers who think that general **learning** mechanisms can accomplish the structuring task (**connectionism, neural constructivism**) and that alternative views commit one to radical concept nativism (see **innateness**). Other arguments include those from **evolution** and the overlap in **brain** areas subserving perceptual discrimination and conceptual thought. However, empiricism runs against the problem, first noticed by **Berkeley**, of abstracting general ideas: how does the mind, on the sole basis of experience, arrive at forming ideas that apply to more than one instance of a category? (For Berkeley, Locke's abstractionist thesis was all the more unacceptable as it entailed the conceivability of such impossible entities as triangles whose sides are neither long nor short.) The same difficulty later arose for **logical positivism** (see **definitional theory**). In order to explain conceptual **content** one must recognise a set of innate primitive (non-decomposable) concepts whose identity remains constant across experiences. For Locke and Hume these were sensory concepts (concepts of colour, taste, shape, etc.), but the difficulty they had with deriving from them the supposedly complex concepts (like those of whole and part) still remains in force.

Further reading: Barsalou (1999); Cowie (1998)

Entailment: logical relation between propositions posing problems for theories of **rationality** and the map-theory of **analytic functionalism**. If someone believes that P and that Q, and (P&Q) entail R, they must believe R (*closure principle*), but people sometimes fail to do so: one may believe that radios are electric devices and that electric devices must not be immersed in water and yet try to clean a radio by placing it in water. If beliefs represented like maps, people would be able to know the consequences of their beliefs (the problem of belief under entailment).

Epiphenomenal: having no causal powers.

Epiphenomenalism: the view that mentality is a causally inert by-product or *epiphenomenon* of **brain** processes. Although mental phenomena are caused by brain processes, they cannot themselves be causes of anything. Epiphenomenalism arose in the late nineteenth century when the acceptance of the **causal closure of the physical** made it difficult to find room for the *conscious* **mind** of **Cartesian** substance **dualism** in the scientific picture of the world. It was defended by Shadworth Hodgson, William Kingdon Clifford, Henry Maudsley and Thomas H. Huxley who compared **consciousness** to the steam-whistle produced by the working of a locomotive engine but having no effect on its machinery. Epiphenomenalism is counterintuitive: it implies that **pain** does not make us wince, that no intentional **action** is possible and that **mental events** cannot become objects of **memory** and **knowledge**. Besides, as **James** noted, it seems incompatible with the theory of **evolution**: why should conscious **mental states** have evolved at all? *Classical epiphenomenalism* does not fall within the province of **physicalism**, for it does not identify even mental events with brain events. In the 1980s, the term, however, began to be used somewhat differently in discussions of **anomalous monism** and **non-reductive physicalism** generally, when the causal efficacy of **mental properties** was put at stake. Today, epiphenomenalism is much at issue in debates about 'conscious free **will**' and **phenomenal consciousness**.

Further reading: Huxley (2001)

Epistemology: the study of the nature and possibility of knowledge.

Error, Problem of see **Misrepresentation, Problem of**

Essential Property: a property which an individual or kind could not have failed to have, which it has in every **possible world** and without which it would cease to exist. Thus having no electric charge is an essential property of neutrons.

Essentialism: the view that things have **essential properties** that make them be what they are. *Metaphysical essentialism* is the term for **Kripke**'s and **Putnam**'s extension of the **causal theory of reference** to **natural kind** terms like 'gold' or 'tiger' whose reference is fixed by the application of a term to a sample of stuff or an animal.

Observational **accidental properties** are usually involved in reference-fixing ('sparkles' or 'is orange with stripes'), but the mechanisms of reference are such that they presuppose that certain kinds of things have 'hidden essences' to be discovered one day. Although we think of cats as animals, it may turn out that they are really robots from Mars. But we will continue to refer to them as 'cats' instead of concluding that cats do not exist (we will simply stop thinking of them as animals). There exists a *division of linguistic labour*: you may not be able to tell a beech from an elm, but because there are experts in your linguistic community, you know that 'beech' and 'elm' have different reference and, if necessary, you may defer to them on that matter. *Psychological essentialism* is the view that people's understanding of natural kind terms indeed involves belief in hidden essences. Thus both adults and older children agree that a racoon made to look and smell like a skunk will not become one, although similar conceptual transformations of artefacts are believed to involve identity changes. Essentialistic thinking may be a universal feature of our **tacit knowledge** of the world.

Evolution: genetic modification of populations over time resulting from small genetic mutations and organisms' interaction with the environment. Migrations place populations into different environmental conditions, and natural selection operating on them results in the spread of genetic material from individuals with the highest reproductive success rates. Today's evolutionary theory differs from that of Charles Darwin (1809–82) who originated it, and a recent renewal of Darwinism (**adaptationism**) continues to provoke controversy. Its critics do not deny that there are **adaptations**, but emphasise the possibility of saltational change. *Saltations* are single genetic mutations producing large effects on an organism's *phenotype* (its physical and physiological features defined by the expression of its genotype in a specific environment), and creating, in Richard Goldschmidt's phrase, 'hopeful monsters'. They are due to mutations of homeotic genes regulating early development. These ideas were developed by Stephen Jay Gould (1941–2002) who noted lack of evidence for intermediate species in the fossil record. Together with Richard Lewontin he coined the term *spandrels* for those features of organisms that, like the spandrels of San Marco Cathedral in Venice which are necessary to support the dome but also bear magnificent mosaics, are by-products of architectural constraints (the body plan, *Bauplan*). Together with Elizabeth Vrba he coined the term *exaptation* for features that evolve for one purpose and are then co-opted for a different purpose (bird feathers evolved for thermoregulation and were co-opted for flight).

Further reading: Gould and Lewontin (1979)

Evolutionary Psychology: a movement in psychology originated by Leda Cosmides and John Tooby. It opposes the Standard Social Science Model according to which individual **minds** contain no domain-specific **representations** at birth (**empiricism**) and are moulded by society through **learning** (sometimes it even holds that **intelligence** or **personality** have no biological determination). Evolutionary psychologists argue that human **cognitive architecture** must be understood in light of its evolutionary history and advocate for (1) the **computational theory of mind**, (2) **innateness**, (3) **massive modularity** and (4) **adaptationism**. The **mind** is composed mostly of innate domain-specific computational mechanisms (modules) that were shaped by natural selection to deal with recurrent **information**-processing problems encountered by humans when they lived in hunter-gatherer societies (the Pleistocene adaptive environment). Although evolutionary psychology down-plays the environment's contribution to individual development, suggests that each kind of problem requires a computational mechanism of its own, diminishes the role of general reasoning abilities and views every mental feature as an adaptive trait contributing to individuals' reproductive success, understood more broadly as a study of stable cognitive and behavioural patterns from the point of view of their **evolution**, it is a viable strategy in **animal cognition** and **cognitive psychology** research.

Further reading: Cosmides and Tooby (1992)

Exaptation see **Evolution**

Exemplar Theory: a psychological theory of **concepts** according to which concepts are sets of exemplars of a category. But although people's memories store **representations** of particular instances, the theory does not explain their **categorisation**.

Explanatory Gap: Joseph Levine's term for the view that nothing known about the physical world can explain **phenomenal consciousness**. Some philosophers believe that the gap cannot be closed because the existence of *qualia* cannot be deduced from any physical facts.

Further reading: Levine (1983)

Extended Mind: the view that one's environment is constitutive of one's cognitive processes (Andy Clark, Michael Wheeler, John Haugeland). As is the case with other **embedded cognition** theories, its proponents lay stress on **embodiment**, the role of **perception** as providing possibilities for **action**, and the understanding of **intelligence** in terms of real-time success of action. It also holds that artefacts are literally constitutive of people's **mental states:**

your mobile phone forms part of your memory for telephone numbers, and its contents constitute in part your beliefs involving these numbers. Minds extend into the environment and **cognition** does not all happen in the head ('active **externalism**'). Human cognition evolved with the development of tools and technologies, of which language is the most important. Extended mind theorists mostly accept **connectionism** as their theory of **cognitive architecture** and **pragmatism** about **concepts**. The problem, though, is how to understand their thesis nonmetaphorically (for example, what are the boundaries of the extended mind?). Extended mind/**dynamical systems** theories were also proposed for **consciousness**. Thus Susan Hurley argues that action is essential to the **unity of consciousness** and that consciousness is neither in the brain nor in subjective awareness.

Further reading: Clark (1997); Hurley (1998)

Extension: the set of all things that a predicate or **concept** is true of. Thus the extension of 'cat' are all and only cats. Two predicates or concepts with the same extension are *coextensive*.

Externalism: the view that **intentional states** (beliefs, desires, etc.) have **broad content**, that is **content** that constitutively depends on one's environment. Externalism stems from **Putnam**'s **Twin-Earth** argument which many found convincing. But the relational nature of intentional states as understood by **folk psychology** seems to make them ill-suited for scientific psychology and the **computational theory of mind** because only those states that are intrinsic to individuals (supervene on their neurophysiology) can enter into causal interactions with each other and be causes of behaviour (the local character of causation). This makes many philosophers accept **internalism**, while others argue that psychological explanation can accommodate broad content because (1) **special sciences** include relational properties in their causal explanations (Tyler Burge, Lynn Rudder Baker); (2) even basic sciences formulate laws with reference to background conditions; (3) **information** carried by organisms' psychological states is a function from their environments (**informational theory of content**); (4) the content of psychological states is determined by their evolutionary history (**teleological theory of content**); (5) rational explanation of **action** requires that the content of intentional states depend in part on their relations to the outside world (Christopher Peacocke, Timothy Williamson). However, as most externalists accept the **representational theory of mind** (but see **demonstrative content**), this allows internalists to argue that, although relevant to causal explanation, broad content is not involved in particular instances of **mental causation**.

Further reading: Burge (1986)

Factive see **Propositional Attitudes**

Faculty Psychology: the view that the **mind** is divided into separate faculties or capacities (perception, memory, imagination, judgement) developed by Franz Joseph Gall (1759–1828) into *phrenology* – the theory that different faculties have discrete **brain** localisation and their prominence correlates with cranial prominence (bumps on the skull).

Feelings see **Sensations**

Fictionalism: the strong version of **instrumentalism** according to which there are no such things as beliefs and desires, that they are merely fictions for predicting behaviour, convenient in everyday life but unacceptable in science.

First-Person Authority: the idea, deriving from **Descartes**, that one's thoughts or experience can be known only from the first-person but not the third-person perspective.

Fodor, Jerry A. (b.1935): American philosopher, the author of the **language of thought** hypothesis. Fodor is thus one of the main defenders of **realism** about **folk psychology**, and to show how beliefs and desires can be genuine causes of behaviour, that is have irreducible causal powers, he developed an influential version of **non-reductive physicalism** (**special sciences** argument). He is a proponent of representational nativism (see **innateness**) and the originator of **informational atomism**. His work on the **modularity** of mind inspired numerous investigations, although he is an ardent critic of **massive modularity**, the extent of the **computational theory of mind** and **connectionism**.
    Further reading: Fodor (2000)

Folk Psychology (belief-desire, intentional, propositional attitude psychology): the common-sense explanation of people's behaviour out of their beliefs and desires (and other **intentional states**). The central tenet of folk psychology is that intentional states have *causal* and *semantic* properties: they cause behaviour in virtue of their **content** ('Why did John come to the lecture theatre on Friday?' 'Because he wanted to listen to Professor N and believed that the lecture would be given there'). Folk psychology thus has impressive predictive and explanatory power. The view that it is largely true is captured in the **representational theory of mind** but is denied by **eliminative materialism**.

Whether in understanding other people's behaviour we indeed employ a folk psychological theory is the issue addressed by **theory of mind** debates.

Frame Problem: a major problem for **artificial intelligence** and the **computational theory of mind**. In doing science and in our everyday life we constantly come across situations when we need to update our beliefs upon receiving new **information** and make decisions about all sorts of problems. Even when one decides whether to take an umbrella or not, knowing that it will rain, all sorts of reasons can bear on the final decision (its colour clashes with one's outfit). Similarly, what modifications one makes to one's beliefs upon learning, say, about the discovery of **mirror neurons** depends on numerous factors. Our reasoning is affected by *global* considerations of *relevance* and *context-sensitivity* (there is nothing in an individual belief itself to show when it may become relevant). Given the algorithmic nature of computational processes, the problem is how to 'frame' the relevant sets of beliefs or limit search spaces. The problem becomes especially acute when one considers the relation between the computational theory of mind and **modularity**. To describe a domain computationally one must specify a clear computational task to be carried out. For this the domain must be restricted with respect to the input it can process (it must be *informationally encapsulated*). This realisation ensures the success of **Marr**'s theory of **vision** (although it poses the **binding problem**). However, general reasoning cannot be so restricted. This, arguably, does not show that thinking is not **computation**, but all current approaches (**heuristics**, **connectionism**, quantum computation) are problematic. Some researchers now believe that **emotions** may be nature's solution to the frame problem.

Further reading: Minsky (forthcoming)

Frege, Gottlob (1848–1925): German mathematician, the founder of modern **logic**. His philosophy of language is of central importance to discussions of **intentionality** and mental **content**. Frege noticed a peculiar asymmetry between such identity statements as 'Hesperus is Hesperus' and 'Hesperus is Phosphorus' (Hesperus is also called 'the evening star', and Phosphorus 'the morning star'). Although they are about the same object, the planet Venus, they differ in their informational content or *cognitive meaning*. It is possible for someone to believe rationally that Hesperus is bright without believing that Phosporus is bright. And in ascribing beliefs we can truthfully say 'Theo believes that Hesperus is bright' but not 'Theo believes that Phosphorus is bright' (*opacity* of belief ascription). How can identity statements be both true and informative and how can one have distinct beliefs about the same object? This is known as the *Frege problem* and in 'Über Sinn und Bedeutung' (1892) Frege offered a solution to it by distinguishing between **sense** (*Sinn*) **and reference** (*Bedeutung*). The reference of an expression is the object it denotes, and its sense is the **mode of presentation** of the reference. 'Hesperus is bright' and 'Phosphorus is bright' express different propositions because they have different senses. In belief ascription contexts like 'Theo believes that Hesperus is bright' the reference of the expression ('Hesperus') shifts so that it does not have its ordinary reference (the planet Venus) but refers instead to its ordinary sense (or mode of presentation of the object referred to by the expression ordinarily).

Further reading: Frege (1960)

Freud, Sigmund (1856–1939): Austrian psychologist, the founder of psychoanalysis. On the basis of his study of psychological disorders Freud postulated a tripartite structure of the **mind**: the conscious mind, the *preconscious* (the part of the mind whose **contents** can become available to **consciousness**) and the **unconscious** (the part containing repressed thoughts and memories that people cannot bring to conscious awareness). Later Freud introduced the parallel categories of the id (the part of the mind driven by instinctual needs and contradictory impulses), the ego (the part responsible for representing the external world and unifying mental processes) and the phylogenetically recent superego (the source of norms of behaviour). The ego, torn by the id's **passions**, the external world and the superego, may break into anxiety, and psychoanalysis must strengthen it by making it take over the unconscious. Psychoanalysis involves the analyst suggesting topics to a patient for 'free association', which the analyst then interprets trying to uncover ideas dominating the patient's unconscious. The method and the overemphasis on suppressed sexual desires were largely discredited, but Freud's impact on **philosophy of mind** should not be underestimated. Freud questioned the assumption that 'consciousness alone is mental', thus influencing **logical behaviourism**, but he also anticipated the ideas of **modularity** and the **intentional** character of non-conscious processes like **dreaming**. Although his notion of the unconscious is controversial, some data support the idea of **memory** repression by executive control mechanisms.

Further reading: Freud (1962)

Functional Role Semantics (FRS, conceptual, inferential, computational role semantics): a theory of **content** according to which the content of a mental **representation** (belief, **concept**) is constituted by its role in reasoning, its inferential or causal relations to other representations. FRS is a consequence of extending **functionalism** about **mental states** to the explanation of how **intentional states** like beliefs and desires acquire their content. It is the most commonly held theory of content whose proponents include Gilbert Harman, Ned Block, Michael Devitt, Brian Loar and William Lycan (although their views differ as to whether it is the **language of thought** or an internalised public language that is the representational medium). Other motivations for FRS include: **Wittgenstein's** and **Sellars'** philosophy of language; **Frege's** consideration that reference alone is insufficient to explain the **cognitive** roles of beliefs (Christopher Peacocke); the consideration that the meaning of logical connectives ('and', 'or') is constituted by the inferences they warrant; and the intuition that the content of many abstract concepts like INFINITY is fixed only by their roles in reasoning. Objections include the problem of **holism** (interdependency of all concepts), the lack of an explanation of representations' informational content, and **Twin-Earth** examples which suggest that functional identity does not entail the identity of contentful states. This led to the development of **molecularism** and **two-factor theories**.

Functionalism: the view that **mental states** are constituted by the totality of their functional or causal relations with other mental states, sensory inputs and behavioural outputs. Thus being in **pain** is constituted by detecting a noxious stimulus, feeling anxious, thinking that something is wrong with one's health, saying 'ouch', etc. Functionalism is the most widely held view on the **mind–body problem**, but functional understanding of mental states allows for two different positions in their relation to **physicalism: machine functionalism** and **analytic functionalism**. However, both positions have to deal with the problem of *qualia* (absent *qualia*, inverted spectrum) which suggests that functional identity does not entail qualitative identity. Other approaches include **homuncular** and teleological functionalism. The term 'functionalism' is also used for functional role semantics.

Further reading: Block (1978); Lycan (1987)

Gestalt: perceived configuration arising from a spatial arrangement able to give rise to different interpretations. If you look at an arrangement of lines and see a human face, this representation has a gestalt quality (due to the brain's tendency to compensate for degenerate stimuli). Gestalt or figure-ground switching, as in the famous duck-rabbit switch, poses questions about the nature of visual consciousness and the mind's structuring of perceptual experience. The school of Gestalt psychology, founded by Max Wertheimer, Kurt Koffka and Wolfgang Köhler in 1910, rejected associationism and held that psychological structures generally are more than sums of their parts. Although their view that gestalts exist in the world proved erroneous, their study of visual illusion was an important contribution to perception research.

Gettier Cases: counterexamples to the view that knowledge is justified true belief presented by Edmund Gettier. Thus you may justifiably believe that someone likes dogs from seeing him give a dog a piece of meat and your belief may turn out to be true, but on this particular occasion the person gave the dog the meat with a soporific inside so as to burgle its owners' house. You have a justified true belief but not knowledge.

Further reading: Gettier (1963)

Ghost in the Machine see Ryle, Gilbert

Gibsonianism see **Direct Perception**

GOFAI: Good Old-Fashioned **Artificial Intelligence.**

Grandmother Cells see **Neurons**

Grice, H. Paul (1913–88): British philosopher, the author of intention-based semantics and theory of conversational implicature. Proponents of the **informational theory of content** make use of his notion of 'natural meaning'. The word 'mean' has different senses and the sense of 'natural meaning' ('indicator-meaning') can be detected in such ordinary sentences as 'These spots mean measles' or 'Smoke means fire'. Non-natural meaning is conventional meaning.

   Further reading: Grice (1957)

Hallucination: the experience of having a **perception** of a real-world object when no such object is being perceived (Macbeth seeing a bloody dagger in front of him).

Hebb, Donald O. (1904–85): Canadian psychologist who argued that to understand how the **brain** subserves psychological functions is to understand how it represents external events (**learning** and **memory**). He suggested that brain **representations** are groups of simultaneously active interconnected **neurons** (*cell assemblies*). If the activation of an assembly is sufficiently long, connections between its neurons become strengthened ('neurons that fire together wire together'). He also suggested that such representations are distributed among cell connections and that the same cells participate in subserving **perception** and memory storage.

Further reading: Hebb (1949)

Heterophenomenology see **Dennett, Daniel C.**

Heuristic: a method of solving problems for which there are no algorithms or which can be solved more quickly if one bypasses exhaustive serial search. Heuristics underlying realistic decision-making (like the recognition heuristic) are studied by theories of bounded **rationality**. Some researchers in **artificial intelligence** believe that heuristic problem-solving may provide a general theory of human **cognition**. But there is a question whether heuristics can circumvent the **frame problem**: if a number of heuristics can be applied to the same problem, then the decision which heuristic to apply is itself sensitive to a system's global properties.

Further reading: Gigerenzer et al. (1999)

Higher-Order Theories: representational theories of **consciousness** which identify it with reflexive or monitoring consciousness. We often speak of conscious **mental states** as states that we are aware of being in. According to the *higher-order thought* (HOT) theory (David Rosenthal, Peter Carruthers), one's mental state M is conscious if it is accompanied by a thought that one is in M, arrived at non-inferentially. Thus being in **pain** is a conscious state for you if you have the thought that you are in pain and did not infer that thought from other thoughts or observation of your behaviour. But this account appears to deny consciousness to infants and animals because they cannot have higher-order thoughts. Thus the *higher-order perception* (HOP) theory which understands the accompanying **representation** as internal scanning similar to **perception** may seem preferable (**Locke, Armstrong,** William Lycan). But that raises the question of what this inner sense is. Besides, both theories must solve the ubiquity problem (if such representations were sufficient for consciousness, computers would be conscious too).

Further reading: Lycan (1996); Carruthers (2000)

Hobbes, Thomas (1588–1679): English philosopher, a defender of **materialism**. Hobbes held that mental processes can be explained in mechanical terms of adding and subtracting quantities in the **brain** (anticipating the **computational theory of mind**).

Further reading: Hobbes [1651] (1957)

Holism: the view that the whole has priority over its parts. *Confirmation holism* formulated by French physicist Pierre Duhem (1861–1916) and Willard van Orman **Quine** is the thesis that scientific theories stand the tribunal of evidence as whole systems of beliefs. But holism about belief confirmation must be distinguished from *semantic holism*, the thesis that the **content** of a **concept** depends on the concept's place within the whole system of beliefs. Semantic holism is motivated by the view in philosophy of language that the meaning of a sentence, hence a word, depends on its role in a language (often the combination of confirmation holism with **verificationism** about meaning), and the view that **mental states** are individuated by their functional roles (**functionalism**). *Holism of the mental* seems highly plausible: if someone has the belief that there is milk for the coffee in the fridge, they must have a whole lot of beliefs about fridges, coffee, milk and relations between them. But if this entails semantic holism, something seems to be wrong, for it follows that no two people, nor the same individual at different times, share concepts. This conclusion appears counterintuitive: people can debate, for example, whether humans are animals or not, but if their concept HUMAN depended on their whole systems of beliefs, they would not be even talking about the same thing. Semantic holism thus leads to **scepticism** about **folk-psychological** generalisation (**interpretivism, eliminativism**), and to avoid it one might consider **atomism** and **molecularism**.

Further reading: Fodor and Lepore (1992)

Holistic: sensitive to the global properties of a system as a whole.

Homuncular Functionalism: William Lycan's term for **Dennett**'s view that the **intentionality** of complex systems can be explained functionally by decomposing them into hierarchically organised subsystems ('homunculi').

Homunculus Argument see **Ryle's Regress**

Hume, David (1711–76): Scottish philosopher, a major proponent of **naturalism**. Hume was the first to propose the use of empirical methods in studying the **mind**, by which he understood discovering general truths about the way humans think, feel and act (**empiricism, representationalism**). Hume distinguished between sensory *impressions* (perceptual **representations** under which he also included **sensations** and **emotions**) and **ideas** deriving from them. Operating on individual impressions **imagination** abstracts general ideas of things, combines simple ideas into complex ones and forms associations between them (**associationism**). However, there are no grounds for thinking that reason can be trusted to reveal the nature of things, and all ideas reflecting matters of fact must be traceable to impressions. This **scepticism** underlies Hume's *projectivism* about **colour**, causality and the **self**.

As we get no impressions of causal connections, causation is the notion the mind projects onto 'loose and separate' events as a matter of habit. And as there is no necessary connection between events, we cannot know that future patterns will follow past patterns and believe justifiably in **causal laws** of nature (Hume's problem of induction). Hume's scepticism also extends to his views on **passions** and the **will**. The term 'Humean **supervenience**', coined by **Lewis**, refers to the view that everything supervenes on the spatio-temporal arrangement of local intrinsic properties.

Further reading: Hume [1748] (1994)

Husserl, Edmund (1859–1938): German philosopher, the founder of **phenomenology**. Husserl held that the aim of phenomenology is to discover the preconditions of experience and reason through a first-person descriptive study of **consciousness**. **Intentionality**, or 'consciousness of', the creation of senses in mental acts which transcends 'experiential givenness' can be studied in abstraction from the actual existence of things (both veridical **perception** and **hallucination** exhibit intentionality). In *Ideas*, his major work, he describes phenomenology as a pure science of essences (an eidetic science), which relates to empirical psychology as geometry to natural sciences. He denounces **naturalism** and the naive natural attitude which unreflectingly posits material objects. The phenomenological attitude, in contrast, involves the exercise of *epoché*, the systematic *bracketing* of all assumptions about the external reality, so that phenomenological reduction could reveal the essences of pure mental processes. Husserl maintains that every intentional process comprises immanent to it *hyle* (uninterpreted **sense-data**) and *noesis*, an act of sense-bestowal, the structuring of hyletic moments by noetic components. Parallel to *noesis* is *noema*, which is not inherent to mental processes. The full *noema* of an intentional process includes a **content** or matter (the noematic what) and its mode of givenness or quality (given in perception, liking, judgement, certainty). In the case of tree-perception, its *noema* is the 'perceived tree as perceived'. As the phenomenological residium discovered by **transcendental** reduction, *noemata* are abstract entities or senses determining objects of possible experiences. This transcendental **idealism** was rejected by other phenomenologists, and in his later work Husserl emphasised the role of intersubjectivity in constituting objects of our life-world (*Lebenswelt*).

Further reading: Husserl [1913] (1982)

Idealism: the view that everything existing is mental in nature. Idealism is traced to **Plato**'s theory of **universals** as preceding things, the view later developed by **Leibniz, Kant, Frege** and **Husserl**. But this is **transcendental** idealism which does not deny the existence of the physical world and must be distinguished from the *subjective idealism* of **Berkeley** (usually referred to as 'idealism'), according to which things exist only inside the **mind**. It is further distinguished from the *absolute idealism* of Hegel and other nineteenth-century idealists.

Ideas: elements of thought, **concepts**. The notion exhibits a duality between ideas as ideal abstract entities which can be apprehended by the **mind** (transcendental **idealism**) and ideas as entities within the mind. Early modern **representationalism**, modelling thinking on **perception**, viewed ideas as objects present to the mind or mental images ('seeing in the mind's eye').

Identity, Numeric versus **Qualitative:** two things are qualitatively identical when they share all their properties. They are numerically identical when they are one thing rather than two.

Identity Theory (type–type or mind–body identity theory): a species of **physicalism,** the view that every **mental property** is identical with some physical (**brain**) property. First suggested by E. G. Boring in 1933, it was developed in the 1950s by U. T. **Place** and J. J. C. **Smart** in Australia, and Herbert Feigl in the USA, supplanting **dualism** and **behaviourism.** Later the identity thesis was elaborated in the **causal theory of mind.** Prior to its appearance, it was commonly thought that identity statements express necessary a priori truths. Influenced by scientific developments, identity theorists argued that statements with psychological terms ('**consciousness** is a brain process', '**pain** is C-fibres firing') are no different from statements like 'lightning is electrical discharge' and similarly express contingent a posteriori identities to be established by empirical investigation. Other arguments included considerations of simplicity, parsimony, **unity of science** (see **Nagelian reduction**) and avoidance of **nomological danglers.** The theory lost some of its appeal in the 1970s due to **Kripke's** analysis of identity, arguments from *qualia*, the anomalousness of the mental and **multiple realisability.** This led many philosophers to **functionalism,** whereas others turned to **eliminative materialism.** Still, the identity theory is a powerful view, and it was recently resurrected in the **phenomenal concepts** approach which became known as *new wave materialism* or *a posteriori physicalism.*

Illusion: the instance when the perceived object appears other than it really is (you thought your shirt had spots on it, but they really were patches of light). The argument from illusion (generally, all kind of perceptual error including **hallucination** and perceptual relativity, when an object appears different from different perspectives) was already used in **ancient philosophy** as an argument for **scepticism**, but is usually traced to **Berkeley**. The possibility of illusion and the subjective indistinguishability of illusory and veridical experiences leads indirect **representationalism** and the **sense-datum theory** to posit intermediary mental entities which constitute the immediate objects of perception. This conclusion may be avoided if one treats illusion as an instance of misrepresentation parasitic on veridical **perception**. There is also an issue of persistent illusions like the Müller-Lyer illusion (two lines of equal length but with outward or inward directed arrows at their ends appear unequal) where no amount of **knowledge** can make the illusory experience disappear. They pose questions about the interaction between external world input and internal processing constraints in producing perceptual experience (**gestalt** perception, perceptual completion phenomena).

Further reading: Wade (2004)

Image Theory: the view that **ideas** (**concepts**) are mental images. Already found in **Aristotle**, it is particularly associated with **Hume**. Despite its intuitive attractiveness (if someone asks you to think of a cat, you are likely to experience a cat-image), the theory does not work. Images are like pictures and lack constituent structure to support the **systematicity** of thought: pictures can be cut into pieces any way one likes, but these pieces are not their interpretable parts, because there is no principled way of putting them together to form new pictures. Besides, there are no images for many concepts (negative concepts like NOT-A-CAT or disjunctive concepts like A-CAT-OR-A-DOG), and images themselves require interpretation (the famous duck-rabbit example, discussed by **Wittgenstein**). A more sophisticated modern version of the theory is found in the idea of Karl Pribram that **representation** in the **brain** is holographic in the same way as the **content** that is contributed by individual points comprising a hologram is not fixed but varies depending on its place within the whole. This proposal, however, meets with the same objection from systematicity.

Imagery: the capacity to experience images, have quasi-perceptual experiences. Images can be experienced in all sensory modalities, but discussions usually concentrate on visual images experienced as internal pictures that can be scanned, rotated, zoomed, etc. Imagery is closely connected with **perception**: imagining involves the activation of the visual cortex, although images are usually less determinate in **content** than actual perceptions. It plays an important role in **memory** (spatial recall) and **action** planning (simulating possible experiences off-line). Many discussions concern the issue of whether imagery is based on symbolic **representation** or whether there is a separate kind of imagistic representation. It arose due to Stephen Kosslyn who discovered a timing consistency in mental scanning and rotation experiments: the amount of time that people take to manipulate an image (for example, 'walk' between locations) is directly proportionate to the amount of time similar behaviour would require in actual situations. He concluded that images themselves have spatial properties isomorphic to those of the represented situation and that imagery is not subserved by the symbolic code (in the representation LONDON IS FURTHER FROM GLASGOW THAN EDINBURGH, the distances between symbols are not themselves physically bigger or smaller). This conclusion was questioned by Zenon Pylyshyn who showed that with a different experimental design where subjects are asked to switch quickly between locations the distance effect disappears and may thus be due not to a specific representational medium but to the way subjects gear their imaginings to various tasks.

Further reading: Pylyshyn (2003)

Imagination: historically, the faculty of the **mind** responsible for thinking and **concept** formation (**image theory**). The notion was prominent in theories of **perception** and **epistemology** up to **Kant**, but later it became tied with questions of **creativity**. Today, the imagination is usually understood as a species of thought (thinking of possibilities) which may or may not be accompanied by mental **imagery**.

Indeterminacy: the property characterising those states of affairs that are neither *A* nor *B*. Arguments from our inability to determine what a state is (**epistemology**) to the inherent indeterminacy of that state (**ontology**) are common practice in philosophy. Thus, drawing on the **indeterminacy of translation**, Daniel **Dennett** argues that the problem of functional indeterminacy does not arise for the **teleological theory of content** because there is no fact of the matter which could decide the correct ascription of **content** to sublinguistic **representations**. Although Dennett in right in pointing out the problem that **inscrutability of reference** poses for **naturalised semantics**, it does not follow that **content** itself is indeterminate because **computations** can be carried out only on binary states. The same problem arises for **analytic functionalism** which holds that the content of **intentional states** is indeterminate but that they nonetheless participate in the causation of behaviour (with this view analytic functionalism comes close to **interpretivism**). Appeals to indeterminacy are also found in arguments in favour of **non-reductive physicalism** and free **will** where they are tied with the indeterminacy of the quantum world and the existence of probabilistic **causal laws**. However, the same reasoning should also lead one to conclude the indeterminacy of higher levels of reality. Consider a simple experiment from thermodynamics where a single molecule travels between two communicating vessels. When one closes the passage between them, one cannot say in which of the vessels the molecule is. Does it follow that its position is ontologically indeterminate?

Indeterminacy of Translation: the most famous expression of the idea of **indeterminacy** associated with **Quine** and **Davidson**. The thesis says that the totality of people's linguistic and non-linguistic behaviour leaves it indeterminate what the correct translation of their utterances is. One reason for the indeterminacy of translation is **inscrutability of reference**. Another reason is that rational interpretation of people's behaviour, because of the **holism** of the mental, leaves it open what particular beliefs should be ascribed to them, if any.

Indexical: an expression whose meaning cannot be specified outside a particular context ('I', 'here', 'now', 'today', 'yesterday').

Individualism see **Internalism**

Individuation: establishing what tokens belong to the same type. The problem of individuation is the problem of determining the criteria of identity for things of the same kind.

Information: the interpretable quantity of data transmitted from a source to a receiver along a communication channel. The notions of information theory can be employed for thinking about **content** and mental **representation**. In formulating the **informational theory of content,** Fred **Dretske** modified Claude Shannon's definition of information to account for the informational content of representational states in terms of conditional probabilities. The idea is that a representational state R carries information about something having property P if R is reliably caused by or covaries with the presence of P (the probability that P given R is 1 on the scale from 0 to 1). Since such correlations are found throughout nature (the number of rings on a tree carries information about that tree's age), this notion of information is naturalistic and non-**intentional.** Electrocommunications also provide an analogy for understanding the distinction between *contents* and *vehicles* of representations: in an electrical device the carrier of a signal is the vehicle, the signal it carries is the content and the information carried correlates with changes in the physical state of the carrier.

Informational Atomism: a theory of **concepts** proposed by **Fodor.** It holds that concepts are symbols in the **language of thought** which receive their content only from the **mind**'s causal connections with the environment (**informational theory of content, atomism**). It contrasts with other theories by viewing lexical concepts as primitive or having no internal structure. (As these theories stem from **Frege**'s distinction between **sense and reference,** it denies that concepts have senses but admits non-Fregean **modes of presentation.**) Its opponents object that it cannot explain connections between concepts in thought (but it can employ **Carnap**'s meaning postulates) or their **cognitive** content (the 'Fido'-Fido fallacy: saying that 'Fido' means Fido does not explain how people represent Fido in thought), that it allows for the existence of punctuate minds (minds with only one belief; the problem of the **holism** of the mental) and that it assumes radical concept **innateness.**

Informational Encapsulation see **Modularity**

Informational Theory of Content (informational semantics): uses the notion of **information** to explain naturalistically how **intentional states** can have **content**. Roughly, one can say that a mental **representation** R has F as its content if it carries information about Fs. That is, contents of representations are determined by their causes: for example, the representation CAT is about cats because cats cause it. However, something else may cause CAT to be tokened (the problem of **misrepresentation**). For this reason **Dretske** first restricted content-fixation to covariance during the 'learning period' when systematic tokenings of CAT occur in the presence of cats and errors are corrected. However, it is possible that during this period dogs, had there been any around, would also have caused CAT and that CAT means *cat or dog* (the **disjunction problem**). A different approach ties content-fixation to epistemically optimal or ideal conditions (originated by Dennis Stampe in his *causal theory of content*, defended by Robert Stalnaker and, briefly, by Jerry **Fodor**). Thus the representation CAT is about cats if it systematically covaries with the presence of cats under epistemically optimal conditions (good illumination, suitable distance). This allows for misrepresentation because tokenings that occur in suboptimal conditions do not count. However, different representations require different optimal conditions to fix their content in a determinate way (cats are best seen in good lighting, but fireflies are not). This makes the solution depend on the content of representations and sheds doubt on its being sufficiently naturalistic. These approaches are known as 'type 1 theories', because they tie content-fixation to special types of situations. Other approaches include Fodor's **asymmetric dependence** theory and **Dretske**'s informational-teleological theory.

Innate: not learned.

Innateness: the property in virtue of which certain traits invariably but following a specific course appear in development, not being fully determined by the input from the environment. To understand the idea of innateness one can consider the notions of maturation (one would not say that the emergence of stereopsis at around four months of age is learned from the environment) and critical period (as Torsten Wiesel and David Hubel showed, the central visual pathway of the monkey **brain** is 'wired up and ready to function at birth' but following early visual deprivation within a short period of time the connections will be lost or modified; see also **cognitive ethology**). The resurrection of **rationalism** about **cognition** is largely due to **Chomsky** whose ideas were later confirmed by studies showing dissociation between syntactic **knowledge** and general **intelligence** (the **Williams syndrome**) and Derek Bickerton's research on creole languages (see also **tacit knowledge**). Yet the view that there are innate **representations** in the **brain** continues to remain controversial, especially when it comes to **concept** innateness: how can COMPUTER and SOAP be innate? But one should remember that nativists acknowledge the need for environmental impact, and the real question is whether differences in the conceptual repertoires of different creatures can be explained by differences in their general learning abilities

without presupposing the existence of innate constraints on representations that are potentially available to them.
Further reading: Carruthers et al. (2005)

Input Problem (the chauvinism–liberalism dilemma):   arises for **machine functionalism** with respect to characterising the relevant subset of sensory inputs that an organism must receive in order to have the right functional organisation (for example, to count as a **pain**-feeling organism). If inputs are themselves characterised functionally, then any mindless structure could satisfy the criteria for mentality (see **absent *qualia***). However, if inputs are characterised relative to human physiology, this leads to **chauvinism** by excluding simple organisms and hypothetical beings from having the relevant **mental states**. It is thus unclear how a mental state could be given an adequate functional characterisation.
Further reading: Block (1978)

Inscrutability of Reference: the thesis developed by **Quine** and **Davidson** (see **radical interpretation**) that no empirical evidence available to the radical interpreter can uniquely determine the reference of words used by speakers of a language. Quine considers the case of an interpreter working with a tribe who hears his informant utter 'gavagai' when a rabbit runs past. He cannot know whether his informant refers to the rabbit, an undetached rabbit part or a rabbit time-slice because all these interpretations are compatible with the same assignment of truth-values to the informant's utterances, leaving reference underdetermined. The thesis thus depends on the presupposition that the nature of thought is linguistic, and in his later work Quine explicitly endorses ontological relativity holding that reference is relative to a language. Intrigued by this issue, developmental psychologists began the study of constraints regulating lexical acquisition.

Further reading: Quine (1969)

Instrumentalism: the view of the **mind** according to which questions about the intrinsic nature of **intentional states** (beliefs, desires) do not make sense and one should be concerned only with establishing criteria for their correct attribution as theoretical entities. It is associated with **Dennett**'s conception of the **intentional stance**.

Intelligence: a general ability required for complex **cognitive** tasks like language processing, analogical reasoning, mathematical and logical reasoning, creative reasoning (musical and artistic), theoretical and practical problem-solving, playing chess, etc. Although the term began to be used only in the early twentieth century with the development of mental testing, it shares with its historical predecessors, 'intellect' and 'reason', the features of **rationality**, effectiveness and flexibility. Recently psychologists questioned the assumption of one ability, suggesting that intelligence is multiple and modularised, which would explain the existence of *idiots savants*, people talented in one area like mathematics but otherwise mentally retarded.

Intension: the principle by which things fall under **concepts**, by which concepts that apply to the same things (have the same **extension**) are distinguished (often understood as the function from **possible worlds** to extensions). Thus CREATURE WITH A HEART and CREATURE WITH A KIDNEY have the same extension, but their intensions are different.

Intensional: (1) sensitive to **intensions;** (2) represented as being a certain way, under some aspect. Creatures sensitive to intensional distinctions would distinguish between EQUILATERAL TRIANGLE and EQUIANGULAR TRIANGLE even though all equilateral triangles are necessarily equiangular.

Intensionality: sensitivity to **intensions**. Intensionality(-with-an-s) is considered to be the criterion of **intentionality**(-with-a-t) because only those creatures can be said to have **concepts** or genuine **intentional states** if they can represent, for example, cats qua cats rather than merely respond selectively to cats. The problem of intensionality (the fine-grainedness problem, the problem of grain) arises for **naturalised semantics** because causation, covariation and biological function are too coarse-grained to take care of **intensional** distinctions. That is, the problem is to explain how a mental **representation** R can represent something as F without representing it as G when the properties F and G are equivalent (nomically, metaphysically or logically).

Intention: a mental plan to perform some **action**. Intentions are what makes pieces of behaviour actions of rational thinking agents, and the capacity to form intentions is central to our practical reasoning and **rationality**. As **intentional states**, intentions have satisfaction conditions (they are satisfied if they cause the projected actions). But the *simple view* of intentional action as an action that the agent had an intention to perform poses problems. Thus one may intend to perform an action (increase the company's profits) which, as one knows, will have certain *side effects* (it will squeeze a lot of small companies out of business) but those are not intended by the agent for he has no desire to cause them. Is causing side effects an instance of intentional action? Another problem is that of *deviant causal chains*: an assassin has an

intention to kill a businessman but on his way to the job
he drops a banana skin on which the businessman, taking the same path later, slips, breaks his neck and dies.
The killer has brought about the killing, but was it an
intentional action? Many people feel that the intention
must be connected to the action in the right way to make
it intentional action but this connection is hard to spell
out. This difficulty is discussed by **Searle** in terms of *prior
intention* (preceding action) and *intention-in-action*, the
mental part of one's bodily movement (close to **volition**).

Further reading: Lepore and Van Gulick (1991)

Intentional: (1) exhibiting **intentionality**, representational; (2)
carried out with a certain **intention**.

Intentional Laws see **Causal Laws**

Intentional Object: that which is represented in thought. It
does not have to be a really existing object but neither is
it an entity in the head. **Brentano**'s view of **intentionality**
as a quasi-relation was quite similar to the current view,
but some of his followers, most notably Austrian philosopher Alexius von Meinong (1853–1920), thought of non-
existent intentional objects as in some sense real because
thought can be directed towards them.

Intentional Psychology see **Folk Psychology**

Intentional Realism see **Realism**

Intentional Stance: a strategy that, according to **Dennett**, we
use in explaining and predicting the behaviour of complex systems by attributing to them **intentional states**
like beliefs. Dennett rejects the distinction between original and derived **intentionality**: all attributions of beliefs

and desires are instruments for predicting behaviour (**instrumentalism**). The intentional stance is contrasted with the *physical stance* used to explain systems' behaviour in terms of physical laws and the *design stance* used to explain how designed systems (artefacts, body organs) work. Any complex system's behaviour can be explained with the help of the lower stances but, given our **cognitive** limitations, the intentional stance maximises our predictive power. Thus not only ourselves but computers too can be treated as *intentional systems* (the behaviour of a normally functioning chess-playing computer is more easily predicted when you think of it as 'wanting' to checkmate your king), and Dennett rejects the **Chinese room** argument saying that the system in question is too slow to count as an intelligent thinker. However, Dennett says that his view is not **fictionalism**: beliefs and desires are idealised 'real patterns' discernible through the interpretation provided by the intentional stance (**interpretivism**). This position becomes clearer in his later work where he endorses **adaptationism** to ground the intentionality of complex systems (their optimal design) in the operation of natural selection.

Further reading: Dennett (1987)

Intentional States: those **mental states** that possess **intentionality**, that are directed at the world (beliefs, thoughts, judgements, opinions, desires, wishes, fears, etc.). Beliefs are paradigmatic intentional states: they have **content** (are about things), their content can be stated in a sentence expressing a proposition, they have satisfaction conditions (can be true or false) and they involve a certain psychological attitude. Thus prototypical intentional states are **propositional attitudes**. A central question is whether there really are such mental entities as beliefs and desires which explain people's behaviour in virtue of their content. The positive answer is intentional **realism** (**folk psychology, functionalism**). Anti-realism includes **behaviourism, instrumentalism, fictionalism, eliminative materialism** and **epiphenomenalism**, while **interpretivism** is partly realism and partly anti-realism. **Searle** distinguishes between *directions of fit* and *directions of causation* for intentional states. Thus beliefs and **perceptions** have the mind-to-world direction of fit but the world-to-mind direction of causation, whereas desires and **intentions** have the world-to-mind direction of fit but the mind-to-world direction of causation (intentions cause **actions,** but the world must 'conform' to intention to make it feasible). For Searle, however, intentionality is secondary to **consciousness,** which is an unusual view today because beliefs can obviously be non-conscious, and one can view non-conscious (**unconscious, subdoxastic**) states as intentional or representational. This understanding of intentional states raises important issues about the relation between intentional and **phenomenal** properties of perceptual experiences, **sensations** and **emotions.**

Intentionalism: see **Representationalism about consciousness**

Intentionality: mind's directedness at objects and states of affairs, the property of some **mental states** (thoughts, beliefs, desires) to be about something, their 'aboutness'. Originating in **medieval philosophy**, the term was resurrected by **Brentano** who viewed the 'intentional inexistence of an object' as one of the marks of the mental. This means that **intentional states** always have something as their object (**intentional object**). But this poses the question of the ontological status of intentional objects, for the **mind** can be directed at non-existent things (you can think about the Golden Mountain without there being any in the world). This makes intentionality a peculiar kind of relation (one that does not require the existence of both relata) and the issue was differently addressed by **Husserl**, **Frege** and **Russell**. The relational character of intentionality was then explored in the **causal theory of reference**, and the next step was Roderick Chisholm's view that **intensionality**(-with-an-s) or 'format-sensitivity' is central to intentionality(-with-a-t). Many contemporary theories of intentionality distinguish between *original intentionality* exhibited by human minds and *derived intentionality* that characterises sentences of natural languages. Understanding intentionality in terms of mental **representation**, some philosophers try to find a place for it in the natural world (**naturalised semantics**) whereas others make it dependent on **consciousness** (see **consciousness, theories of**).

Further reading: Chisholm (1957)

Interaction Problem: a problem for **interactionism**, which must explain how the mental, being different in kind from the physical, can nonetheless effect changes in the physical world.

Interactionism (Cartesian interactionist **dualism**): the doctrine originated by **Descartes** that the mental and material substances interact in a certain **brain** location (for Descartes, the pineal gland) through which the **mind** receives **sensations** and initiates voluntary **action**. With the growing realisation that science requires **causal closure of the physical**, interactionism, which was a very widespread view before that time, almost completely disappeared in the twentieth century.

Internalism (individualism): the view that the **content** of **intentional states** (beliefs, desires) relevant to the explanation of behaviour is fully determined by factors internal to an individual. Internalism was originated by **Fodor** (later converted to **externalism**) under the name of *methodological solipsism* as the principle that **cognitive psychology** (and the **computational theory of mind**) should concern itself exclusively with what goes on inside people's heads and disregard their external environment because only internal states can be causes of behaviour and other **mental states**. To resolve the conflict between the relevance of content to behaviour (the **representational theory of mind**) and the **Twin-Earth** argument which shows that intentional states have environmentally dependent **broad content,** one must isolate a special kind of non-relational **narrow content** which wholly depends (supervenes) on an individual's internal states. As a principle of explanation in **cognitive science**, internalism finds support in the **brains in vats** argument and such non-psychological analogies as that to find cure for a burn one does not need to know what caused it but only the local effects it has on the damaged area. A different argument in favour of internalism was offered by **Lewis** and other proponents of **analytic functionalism**. They argue that because our beliefs are largely *de se*, beliefs with narrow content are more fundamental psychologically, and beliefs with broad content can be understood in terms of beliefs with narrow content plus the history of one's causal connections to the world (**deflationism** about broad content). Still another defence of internalism is to question the validity of **Twin-Earth** and arthritis **thought experiments**.

Further reading: Fodor (1980)

Interpretivism (interpretationism): the view that possession of **intentional states** (beliefs, desires) is constituted by the fact that a suitably placed and fully informed interpreter would ascribe them to subjects in order to interpret their behaviour. It opposes the idea of **first-person authority**

and is associated with **Quine**'s and **Davidson**'s theory of **radical interpretation,** and **Dennett**'s conception of the **intentional stance.**

Introspection: observation of one's own **mental states** and processes, 'looking inwards'. Though introspection is often unreliable, and many states and processes are not introspectively accessible (sentence parsing), it remains important in studying **cognition** ('protocol analyses') and, especially so, **phenomenal consciousness.**

Introspective Psychology: the first school of experimental psychology founded by Wilhelm **Wundt** in Germany in the 1860s and developed in the USA by his student Edward B. Titchener who, as some argue, simplified Wundt. By the 1920s it had been superseded by **behaviourism.**

Intertheoretic Reduction: establishment of relations between elements of two theories so that those of the higher-level theory would be explained through those of the lower-level theory. Is called '**nomological** reduction' when it is held that theory construction is inseparable from formulating **causal laws. Nagelian reduction** is often taken as its prototype, but this view is challenged by **new wave reductionism.**

Inverted Earth: Ned Block's argument against **functionalism** and **representationalism about consciousness,** a modification of **inverted spectrum,** pertaining to show that experiences with the same **phenomenal** character may have different functional roles and representational **contents.** Inverted Earth is different from Earth in two respects: (1) all **colours** are complementary to those on Earth (grass is red, the sky is yellow); (2) its inhabitants use inverted colour words ('red' means green). A person from Earth is unknowingly transferred to Inverted Earth and colour inverters are inserted into her eyes. Upon awakening she won't know anything has changed. But as time passes and she gets used to the language and physical environment of that planet, the representational contents of her mental states will become just like those of the other inhabitants (she will start thinking that the sky is yellow). Thus although her *qualia* remain the same, she becomes functionally and representationally inverted relative to her earlier self.

Further reading: Block (1990); Lycan (1996)

Inverted Spectrum (inverted *qualia*): an argument in favour of **colour** subjectivism and against **functionalism**. It is conceivable that two individuals can be functionally identical, even though one of them sees red things as green and green things as red. Thus functionalism cannot explain the **phenomenal** character of experience. However, one may object that there will be functional differences as the two individuals will have different beliefs about colour and their colour words will have different meanings.

Jackson, Frank (b.1943): Australian philosopher, the author of the **knowledge argument** and a proponent of **analytic functionalism**. Until recently he defended the **sense-datum theory** of **perception** and **dualism** about *qualia*. Jackson still holds that knowledge argument must be interpreted ontologically rather than epistemically but thinks that his earlier thesis of non-deducibility is wrong. If physicalism is the most scientifically respectable approach to the **mind**, and a priori entailment the only conceptually sound way of grounding **reduction,** then a priori physicalism must be true and *qualia* must be deducible from physical facts (as liquidity is deducible from molecular structure). The grounds for such reduction are provided by **representationalism about consciousness.**

Further reading: Jackson (2004)

James, William (1842–1910): American philosopher, the founder of American psychology. James's first work was on the theory of **emotions** and criticism of **epiphenomenalism.** In *The Principles of Psychology* (1890) the theme of **consciousness** comes even more to the foreground, and James isolates the permanent flow of experience, 'the stream of consciousness' (opposed to **Wundt**'s 'succession of ideas') as the most concrete fact of which we are aware. He argues that the **unity of consciousness** cannot result from the interaction of many components of a system and concludes that consciousness cannot be distributed over matter ('combination problem'), but he also contemplates the possibility of consciousness in individual **neurons.** Later this led him to **neutral monism** (**Russell**'s term for James's 'radical **empiricism**'), although some researchers argue that sometimes he comes closer to **panpsychism.** James also defended **pragmatism** as the view that beliefs (including religious beliefs) are true if they work.

Further reading: James [1890] (1981); [1912] (1976)

Kant, Immanuel (1724–1804): German philosopher, the founder of critical philosophy. In his later writings, Kant distinguished four types of **knowledge** along the dimensions of a priori, a posteriori, analytic and synthetic.

Analytic a priori judgements, where predicates are 'contained' in their subjects ('father is the male parent') are not informative. It is the synthetic a priori that sets the preconditions and limits of naturalistic inquiry. We have knowledge of things existing in space and time because these two categories and those of object, causation and the experiencing **self** are part of the schema imposed by reason on experience. The sensory *manifold* (physical energies bombarding our senses) is an incoherent flux which becomes experience only when **imagination** (*Einbildungskraft*) synthesises it into **representations** that fall under **concepts**. Because of the **transcendental** nature of the manifold and the categories reason can only deliver knowledge of things as they appear to us (*phenomena*) but not as they are in themselves (*noumena*). On the other hand, without sensory experience no object would be given to us. Thus reason cannot legitimately claim to have any knowledge of those things which have no basis in experience, including reason itself.

Further reading: Kant [1781] (1997)

Kim, Jaegwon (b.1934): American philosopher, initially a major figure in the formulation of the idea of **supervenience** and supervenient causation, then a proponent of **reductive physicalism.** He argues for the **reduction** of intentional **mental properties,** but accepts partial irreducibility of *qualia* and *qualia* **epiphenomenalism.** (differences between *qualia,* like those between the green *quale* and the red *quale* are functionalisable, but their subjective character, like the greenness of green, are not and in that respect they are irreducible).

Further reading: Kim (2005)

KK-Thesis: the thesis that if the subject S knows that P, then S knows that S knows that P.

Knowledge: justified true belief, according to the common view traced back to **Plato**. This view was shattered by **Gettier cases** and recently attacked by Timothy Williamson who argues that no decompositional analysis of knowledge would be correct because of general problems with definitions and the distinct causal connection between knowledge and behaviour. You may have a justified true belief that you need to be at some place at some time (you were provisionally told so and are expected), but without *knowing* that you may well decide not to go. Williamson also holds that knowledge (like other factive **propositional attitudes**) is best understood as a **mental state** with **broad content**. It is a *prime* state that cannot be factorised into external (contributed by the world) and internal (confined to an individual's **mind/brain**) components because it does not allow for any recombination of the two components other than the existing one, which favours **externalism**. Critics object to this analysis of the factorising strategy and point out that, as in the case of **disjunctivism,** the account runs against the problem of introducing radically different explanations for subjectively indistinguishable states of knowledge and not-knowledge.

Further reading: Williamson (2000)

Knowledge Argument: an argument advanced by **Jackson** to show that **physicalism** must be false because **knowledge** of all relevant physical facts throws no light on the qualitative character of experience (*qualia*). Imagine a super-scientist Mary who knows all the physical facts about the **brain** and **colour** vision but has never left her black-and-white room (she has been painted black and white, too). One day she leaves that room and sees the world in its full colour. Does she learn anything new about colour? The answer seems to be yes for she discovers **what it's like** to see red or green. But physicalism cannot allow that Mary acquire any new knowledge. Reactions to the argument include: (1) saying that Mary acquires new **knowledge-how**, but not **knowledge-that**; (2) saying that she acquires new **phenomenal concepts** which constitute new knowledge but pick out the same properties as her old scientific concepts; (3) seeing the problem as misconceived because physicalism is correct for reasons of the **causal closure of the physical** (but Jackson accepted *qualia* **epiphenomenalism**); (4) viewing it as an epistemological, not an ontological problem.

Further reading: Jackson (1982); Ludlow et al. (2004)

Knowledge under Entailment see **Entailment**

Knowledge, Declarative: in psychology, **knowledge** of facts and events stored in declarative **memory** and expressed with the help of declarative sentences.

Knowledge, Procedural: in psychology, **knowledge** of how to execute procedures underlying acquired motor skills, habits and behaviours. It is stored in procedural **memory**.

Knowledge, Propositional see **Knowledge-that**

Knowledge, Tacit see **Tacit Knowledge**

Knowledge-How: the kind of **knowledge** that seems to underlie many of our physical activities and can be stated with the help of a how-clause (Mary knows how to tie her shoes). Arguing that much intelligent human behaviour does not require **knowledge-that** to guide it, **Ryle** postulated knowledge-how, an ability or complex of **dispositions**. Although the dispositional analysis was rejected, some philosophers find the distinction useful and view knowledge-how as extending beyond *procedural knowledge* to include linguistic competence or mathematical proof which is then viewed as a kind of **action** not mediated by internal **representations**. Knowledge-how was also used by Lawrence Nemirow and David **Lewis** as a response to the **knowledge argument**: upon release Mary acquires not some new propositional knowledge, but an ability to recognise, imagine and remember different **colours** (the *ability hypothesis*). One problem with knowledge-how is that it cannot be identified with ability because one may know how to do something while having lost the ability to do it (Carl Ginet). Besides, the analysis of embedded questions reveals no important difference between knowledge-how and knowledge-that. Jason Stanley and Timothy Williamson argue that knowledge-how is a species of knowledge-that involving **demonstrative content** (to know how to do something is to know that w is the way to do it). Thus, if Mary's ability to imagine involves knowledge-how, she must have acquired new knowledge-that.

Further reading: Lewis (1988); Stanley and Williamson (2001)

Knowledge-that: propositional **knowledge** statable with the help of a declarative sentence expressing a proposition (Mary knows that snow is white). The fact that some knowledge is an instance of knowledge-that requires neither that the subject contemplate a proposition prior to initiating an **action** (it may be automatic) nor that they be capable of consciously representing or linguistically expressing the whole sequence of elements constituting such a proposition.

Kripke, Saul A. (b.1940): American philosopher, the author of an important critique of the **identity theory** ('Kripke problem', 'Kripke's modal argument'). Extending his causal theory of reference to natural kind terms (essentialism) and viewing them as *rigid designators* picking out the same objects in all possible worlds, Kripke introduced into philosophy the notion of *a posteriori necessity*. Because theoretical identity statements like 'light is a stream of photons' involve rigid designators, they are a posteriori and necessary (they are necessarily true if shown to be true by empirical investigation). Identity theorists argued that the identifications of mental states with brain states are similar to the identifications of physical science. Kripke objects. The reference of 'light' is fixed by light's accidental property – 'that which helps us see', but 'light is a stream of photons' captures light's essential property. Even if we could not see, or if alien creatures received their visual impressions from sound waves, the reference of our word 'light' would not change. However, things are different with mind–brain identity statements like 'pain is C-fibres firing'. The reference of 'pain' is fixed by pain's essential property because to be pain is to feel like pain. And it is logically possible that C-fibres firing could have existed without feeling like pain or that pain could have existed in the absence of C-fibres firing. But if this were a genuine theoretical identity, it would be necessary. Similar views are developed today by David Chalmers in his theory of phenomenal consciousness.

Further reading: Kripke (1980)

La Mettrie, Julien Offroy de (1709–51): French doctor and philosopher, a defender of materialism. In *L'Homme machine* (1748, *Man a Machine*) he argued that 'irritation' of the nerves can explain both reflexive and intelligent behaviour, in animals and humans.

Language and Thought see **Thought and Language**

Language of Thought (LOT, Mentalese): a hypothesis about the form of mental **representation** advanced by **Fodor**. Noting the sensitivity of **propositional attitudes** (beliefs, desires) to combinatorial structure unaccounted for by **machine functionalism**, Fodor proposed to view them as relations between subjects and mental representations. Thus Mary may believe that she saw a tiger or desire to see one but both these states are about the same thing. The metaphor of *belief* and *desire boxes* captures this aspect of the hypothesis. LOT is the medium of thought which shares important properties with natural language: it contains *symbols* or representational atoms ('words') which, following **recursive** rules, can be put together to form complex representations ('sentences'). LOT is not identical to any natural language but is **innate** and prior to natural language (there must be a representational medium in which one could construct logical forms of such ambiguous sentences as 'the chicken is ready to eat' in order to understand their intended interpretations). A common objection is that LOT cannot explain representation in non-linguistic animals and infra-linguistic infants or low-level perceptual processing because these do not have the form of natural language sentences (hence, *sententialism*). However, the objection is misguided because LOT is not about 'sentences in the **brain**', but about *predication*, the assignment of properties to objects, which characterises all kinds of representation.

Further reading: Fodor (1975)

Learning: the process by which organisms acquire new **knowledge**. There are lots of things we learn and this capacity is essential to our operation in the world. But the debated question is whether the **mind** contains almost no unlearned **representations** (**empiricism**). **Behaviourism** and **interpretivism** hold that associative learning can explain meaning acquisition. However, Paul Bloom showed that acquisition of word meaning by association is characteristic of children with **autism** (if an adults drops a hammer and utters a swear word, they will learn it as meaning 'hammer') but not of normally developing children. The difficulty of understanding **concept** acquisition as learning was emphasised by **Fodor** (anticipated by **Plato**): in concept learning experiments subjects must acquire a non-existent concept by deciding whether instances presented by the experimenter fall under it. With input from the experimenter they soon begin categorising instances correctly. Thus it may turn out that 'flurg' means RED CIRCLE. However, to understand that they had to formulate and confirm hypotheses about the meaning of 'flurg' that could only be done if they already had RED and CIRCLE. Thus it seems that one can acquire simple concepts only if one already has them. With the emergence of **connectionism** theories of learning received a new domain-general mechanism that could account for the acquisition of competences, including syntactic knowledge. Besides, connectionism realises principles of learning in neural systems postulated by **Hebb** (Hebbian learning) and confirmed at the molecular level (long-term potentiation and depression). But as some research suggests, learning by back propagation is neurally unrealistic because it implies that the **brain** implements 'God-like algorithms', is global and slow (whereas organisms can learn from one instance).

Further reading: Elman et al. (1996)

Leibniz, Gottfried Wilhelm (1646–1716): German philosopher and mathematician. Leibniz developed **Descartes'** theory of **ideas**, the notion of substance (denying the existence of the infinitely divisible extended material substance) and the topological conception of reality (proposing the relational understanding of space and anticipating the informational theory of causation). As the creative power actualising possibilities, God cannot allow indeterminate entities, and all real individual things are divisible into further individual things for which there is a complete idea in God's mind such that all properties of a thing can be deduced from it. Because God acts by the *principle of sufficient reason*, the actual world is the best of all **possible worlds** (and all apparently contingent facts are in reality necessary). It is constituted by *monads*: simple, individual, mental, self-sufficient unities (substances) whose modifications are determined by their intrinsic natures and are independent of other things. There is no causal interaction in the world: just as two clocks set a minute apart may appear to be causally interacting when in fact they are not, everything in the world was set in motion by God (the doctrine of *pre-established harmony*, Leibniz's version of **parallelism**). Individual human **minds** are also monads, but ones inherently characterised by perceptual unity and (**self**)**consciousness** which belong to simple, not complex substances: we can imagine constructing a feeling and thinking machine the size of a mill, but walking through it and observing its mechanical operations we would not find anything to explain consciousness (*Leibniz's Mill*). Leibniz was also the inventor of rational calculus (*characteristica universalis*) and a critic of **empiricism**, adding to the *nihil in intellectu* dictum the words *nisi intellectus ipse*: there is nothing in the intellect unless first in the senses *except the intellect itself*.

Further reading: Leibniz [1714] (1989)

Leibniz's Law (identity of indiscernibles): the principle that if *x* is identical with *y*, then *x* and *y* must have all the same properties.

Lewis, David K. (1941–2001): American philosopher, one of the originators of the **causal theory of mind.** Viewing **folk psychology** as a 'term-introducing scientific theory' which explains behaviour in terms of causal roles played by different **mental states,** Lewis argued that rewriting it in a **Ramsey sentence** and adding the requirement of unique realisation for causal roles vindicates the **identity theory** (causal roles corresponding to mental terms can only be occupied by states causally related to behaviour, that is **brain** states). Acknowledging later the possibility that a mental state like **pain** may neither play its typical causal role ('mad pain' which does not cause one to wince) nor have its typical physical realisation due to **multiple realisability** (physically different 'Martian pain') and, contra **Kripke,** embracing the non-rigidity of mental terms, Lewis introduced the notion of *domain-specific* or *restricted identities.* A mental state must be identified with a physical state which realises the appropriate causal role in a limited population. This explains Martian pain, while mad pain can be treated as an exceptional case in members of a population, and mad Martian pain must be evaluated relative to the Martian population. Lewis's analysis originated **analytic functionalism,** though for Lewis the identity thesis was always more important than **functionalism.**

Further reading: Lewis (1972, 1980, 1994)

Locke, John (1632–1704): English philosopher, the founder of **empiricism.** Locke's rejection of innate **ideas** came from his views about the inadequacy of our ideas in moral and legal spheres, but also ideas of secondary qualities like **colour.** His empiricism is thus inseparable from his distinction between **primary and secondary qualities, representationalism** and belief in real essences. Locke argued that the systematic and involuntary character of perceptual experience shows that it must represent an independent world of material objects. The causal relation between the world and the **mind** in **perception** ensures the adequacy of our ideas of primary qualities, but our ideas of secondary qualities are inadequate because they do not capture the real essences of things (still, his position was close to colour **realism,** for he viewed secondary qualities as objective intrinsic powers of objects to produce ideas in the minds of perceivers). Locke also originated the currently most widely held view of **personal identity.**

Further reading: Locke [1689] (1975)

Logic: a formal science of correct reasoning by drawing inferences. Reasoning can be divided into deduction (inferring a conclusion from a set of premises by following rules), induction (coming to a general conclusion on the basis of instances) and **abduction.** The origins of logic may be traced to **Aristotle,** but modern logic is credited to **Frege** who invented the first propositional calculus (the study of relations among propositions) and predicate calculus (the study of relations among statements in which properties are predicated of objects). The calculi, subsequently elaborated by **Russell** and philosophers of **logical positivism,** are employed in **philosophy of mind** in discussions of **intentionality** and **representation** (the problems of belief under **entailment** and **intensionality**). Logic also underlies the **computational theory of mind:** in drawing deductive inferences people often manage to arrive at true conclusions when starting from true premises. This property of truth-preservation belongs to the *form* of propositions and inference may thus be implemented in machines. Modal logic, which uses the notion of **possible worlds** to study necessity and possibility (invented by **Kripke** and Stig Kanger), is invoked in discussions of the **mind–body problem.** But logic is a prescriptive, not a descriptive science: it tells one nothing about the extent to which human reasoning follows **content**-insensitive formal rules. This issue is raised in recent theories of **rationality** as psychological evidence suggests that human reasoning is not formally logical.

Logical Behaviourism (analytic behaviourism): the philosophical variety of **behaviourism** influenced by **logical positivism**'s distrust of unobservables. Among its proponents were **Ryle**, Hempel, **Quine** and **Wittgenstein**. It was weakened by the same factors as **methodological behaviourism**, but also its inability to provide behavioural necessary and sufficient conditions for being in some mental state, the insufficiency of behaviour for mentality (a brainless puppet controlled from Mars may exhibit behaviour indistinguishable from ours), the irreducibility of **mental states** to behavioural **dispositions** (one can feel **pain** without showing it in verbal or nonverbal behaviour), its denial of **first-person authority** over one's internal states (one can know how one is feeling upon waking up when one has not moved around for one's behaviour to 'feedback' this knowledge) and the untenability of the view that introspective reports are not reports of internal states of **consciousness** (the point made by the **identity theory**). In the 1960s behaviourism was supplanted by **functionalism**, but its influence is felt in functionalism's thesis that tendencies to behave are constitutive of mental states. It is also felt in any position that denies **representations** or rejects **realism** about **intentional states** by coming close to *supervenient behaviourism*, the view that mental facts supervene on behavioural dispositions: that two persons with identical behavioural dispositions are identical psychologically.

Further reading: Putnam (1968)

Logical Positivism (logical empiricism): philosophy of science developed in the 1920–30s by members of the Berlin Society for Scientific Philosophy and the Vienna Circle. The latter included Moritz Schlick (the founder), Rudolf **Carnap**, Otto Neurath, Kurt Gödel and Herbert Feigl who were in regular contact with Carl Hempel, Alfred Tarski, Alfred Julius Ayer, Ludwig **Wittgenstein** and Karl Popper. Striving to free science from metaphysics, they endorsed radical **empiricism** concluding that the only meaningful scientific statements are either analytic (logically true or false) or testable by observation (synthetic a posteriori). This resulted in **verificationism** about meaning, although the group was split between **phenomenalism** and **realism** about material objects. The logical positivist programme was abandoned with the realisation that scientific hypothesis confirmation is **holistic** and that science proceeds by postulating entities which are not immediately observable. However, logical positivism had enormous influence on the development of **logic** and conceptual analysis, and its ideal of the **unity of science** remains relevant to current discussions of **physicalism**.

Further reading: Ayer (1959)

Machine Functionalism: (input–output, empirical functionalism or psychofunctionalism): the variety of **functionalism** which identifies **mental states** with higher-order computational or functional states of a system. **Putnam** proposed to view the **mind** as a probabilistic **Turing machine** where transitions between states occur with various probabilities rather than being deterministic. Putnam saw the functional description of the mind in terms of inputs, outputs and mediating internal states as an empirical hypothesis fixing the **extensions** of psychological terms. If the same predicates ('is in **pain**', 'is hungry') may, on the basis of behaviour, be applied to creatures with different physical-chemical organisation, then having a mind is identical with having a certain functional organisation. This is the **multiple realisability** thesis crucial to machine functionalism's idea of *species-independent psychological laws*. But this view poses the **input problem**, which is why although functionalism is often identified with machine functionalism, its present form is closer to a combination of the **computational theory of mind** and **non-reductive physicalism** (see also **silicon chip replacement** for the position known as *causal functionalism*). Early functionalism, focusing on sensory states which probably are unstructured or *monadic*, also had difficulty with **propositional attitudes** which require combinatorial structure ('believes-that-snow-is-white' and 'believes-that-snow-is-wet' cannot be unrelated states) and had to be supplemented with a theory of **convent** (see **functional role semantics**).

Further reading: Putnam (1967)

Machine Table: a table giving a full description of possible states of a finite state machine (a deterministic automaton) specifying what next state it moves to and what output it produces given some input and its current state (think of a coke-vending machine). Any given state of such a machine is exhaustively characterised in functional terms.

Malebranche, Nicolas (1638–1715): French philosopher, a major proponent of **occasionalism**. This metaphysical position was consistent with his acceptance of **Descartes'**

rationalism that he developed into the view that **ideas** are objects in the mind of God.

Further reading: Malebranche [1674–5](1997)

Manifest Image see **Sellars, Wilfrid**

Manifold see **Kant, Immanuel**

Marr, David (1945–80): British psychologist, the author of the leading computational theory of **vision** and three-level analysis of **information**-processing adhered to in **cognitive science**. Marr proposed that the **mind**'s structuring effects on visual experience identified by **Gestalt** psychologists can be accounted for computationally. The visual system's computational task is to create representations of 3-D(imensional) objects from 2-D images on the retina as its input. Retinal stimulations are **representations** of light and intensity values (dark and bright patches) in a 2-D coordinate system. On their basis the visual system computes a primal sketch of surface reflectance changes which then serves as input to the construction of a 2.5-D sketch representing surface depth and contours from the viewing perspective. From this, it constructs a 3-D sketch, which is what we see being aware of the way objects' surfaces are out of view. Discussions of Marr's theory concern the question of how it bears on the explanation of visual **consciousness** and the debate between **externalism** and **internalism**.

Further reading: Marr (1982)

Massive Modularity: the view, central to **evolutionary psychology**, that the **mind** largely consists of domain-specific computational modules. It thus reconsiders **Fodor**'s notion of **modularity** which distinguishes modular input systems from non-modular central reasoning processes.

The clearest candidate for a central module is the cheater-detection module postulated to explain the results of the **Wason selection task** (the **theory of mind** module is another). However, according to Fodor, a cheater-detection *computational module* is impossible because there are no perceptual cues for automatic detection of social exchanges. Steven Pinker objects to this, citing evidence that people tend to interpret movement of dots on a screen in terms of human relations. But there are also general issues regarding the allocation of inputs to non-peripheral modules and the interaction between modules, for the possibility of central modules depends on whether computational modules may *not* be informationally encapsulated (**frame problem**). The idea of massive modularity was partly motivated by the view that general reasoning mechanisms would be overloaded with **information** and be incapable of processing it. However, this may involve a misconstrual of the relation between **innate** structures and the capacity for **learning** and inferencing (consider the capacity of humans and possibly other higher animals to understand that some perceptual experiences are **illusions**). For this reason it may be preferable to view the massive modularity thesis as requiring **Chomsky**'s modules.

Further reading: Samuels (2000)

Materialism: the view that everything existing is material. Historically, that was understood as being matter, the extended substance. As contemporary physics admits of entities that are not material in this sense (like gravitational forces), the term **physicalism** is often preferred today.

Medieval Philosophy (approximately 600–1400): the first merger between **ancient philosophy** and Christianity via Neoplatonism was accomplished by St Augustine of

Hippo (354–430). Neoplatonism (founded by Plotinus, *c*.205–270) reinterpreted **Plato**'s ideas as existing in the mind of the One whose emanation creates the realms of the intellect and the soul; ideas can be grasped by the intellect whereby the immortal soul achieves reunion with the One. Later, Manlius Severinus Boethius (480–524) resurrected the problem of **universals**. But a more philosophically important period began with the establishment of universities in the twelfth century and the spread of **Aristotle**'s philosophy coming from Arabic and Greek sources. A major Arabic influence was Abu Ali Al-Husayn Avicenna (Ibn Sina, 980–1037) whose Neoplatonic Aristotelianism and views on the soul were consonant with the Christian doctrine. The second major influence was Averroës (Ibn Rushd, 1126–98) who opposed Avicenna's interpretation of Aristotle, holding that only individuals have primary existence and that essences are the product of the intellect. He also believed in the eternity of the world, thought that the intellect was a separate entity from the soul rather than its faculty and thus denied personal immortality. His view became known as the doctrine of double truth (different for faith and reason) and was condemned in 1277. The thirteenth century was the heyday of scholastic philosophy which produced St Albert the Great, St Thomas **Aquinas**, Roger Bacon and St Bonaventure, but the fourteenth century brought with it John Duns Scotus and William of Ockham whose work is equally important for understanding the problem of **universals** in its connection with the problem of **intentionality**.

Further reading: Pasnau (1997)

Memory: the **mind**'s capacity to think about past occurrences, to retain learned **information**. Several types of memory are distinguished: *declarative* or *propositional* *memory* (memory for facts and events) is contrasted with *nondeclarative memory* which includes memory for conditioned associations, emotional responses, and *procedural* or *behavioural memory* (memory for skills and behaviours). *Long-term memory* (items stored in it can be recalled months and years after they were registered) is contrasted with *short-term memory* (where items are placed for temporary storage; George Miller showed that short-term memory can simultaneously retain about seven items – 'the magical number seven'). *Explicit memory* (memories that can be acknowledged by subjects) is contrasted with *implicit memory* (memories of which subjects have no awareness but whose existence can be inferred from their improved performance on various tasks). *Working memory* is the storage which contains information relevant to the control of ongoing behaviour. Some researchers hold that higher forms of **self-consciousness** depend on conscious *autobiographical memory* which may require language. Other philosophical issues about memory concern its role in our **personal identity** and limited **rationality**; the problem of **cognitive architecture** and memory storage; the causal theory of memory and the problem of deviant causal chains; and the problem of false memories (relevant to the **externalism–internalism** debate).

Mental Causation: the cornerstone of the **mind–body problem**. **Mental states** are caused by physical happenings in the world (**perception**, upward causation), cause other mental states (thinking, same-level causation) and physical events (downward or topdown causation, **action**). Mental-to-physical causation is particularly problematic for proponents of **non-reductive physicalism** who hold that **mental properties** have real irreducible causal powers (for example, that it is wanting a glass of juice together with believing that there is juice in the fridge that makes one go to the kitchen). The problem of *downward causation* (the *supervenience* or *exclusion argument*) was formulated by **Kim**. Consider the case when a mental event M causes another mental event M*. Non-reductive physicalists accept the **physical realisation principle** or the **supervenience** thesis. Thus M* must be physically realised. So why is M* instantiated? They must say: because one of its physical realisers, P*, is. P* alone is sufficient for the instantiation of M*. Then what is the role of M in causing M*? M* can be instantiated only if P* is. They must now say that M causes P*. This is an instance of downward causation. However, M must also be physically realised. Thus: M is realised by P, P causes P* and M* is realised by P*. But where is the causation of M* by M as such? It appears that mental states qua mental do no causing, and one is forced to chose between **reductive physicalism** and **epiphenomenalism** (or else find a different non-reductivist solution).

Further reading: Heil and Mele (1993); Walter and Heckmann (2003)

Mental Concepts: the **concepts** of perceiving, sensing, feeling, believing, hoping, desiring, etc. that form part of our **folk psychology**. The implicit reference they contain to the **holism** and **rationality** of thought processes is what makes the **mind–body problem** and explanations of their **content** so difficult. But their existence poses even more serious problems for **eliminative materialism**: if mental concepts do not pick out anything real (there is nothing at the level of **brain** activity that, say, corresponds to the belief that it is raining), then what do they pick out and why do we have them? **Searle** notes that even if the entities posited by folk psychology are unsuited for doing science, it does not follow that they do not exist, for otherwise one would also have to deny existence to tennis rackets or golf clubs. Similarly, Stephen Stich observes that given the **causal theory of reference** even a false theory can refer to existing entities: if members of a community believe that stars are gods, it only follows that they are mistaken about stars, not that they fail to refer to stars.

Further reading: Stich (1996)

Mental Content see **Content**

Mental Events: particular happenings in the **mind.**

Mental Object: an entity existing in the **mind,** 'a thing in the head'.

Mental Properties: mental kinds or types such as *being in pain* or *believing that it is raining* that can be instantiated by different individuals on different occasions. Like **mental states** they can be divided into **phenomenal** and **intentional.**

Mental Representation see **Representation**

Mental States: psychological states like perceiving, remembering, believing, desiring, hoping, intending, feeling, experiencing, etc. that individuals can be in. The main distinction is between **intentional** and **phenomenal** states. Other distinctions include: **occurrent** and **dispositional**, perceptual and conceptual, **doxastic** and **subdoxastic**, conscious and **unconscious** states.

Mentalese see **Language of Thought**

Merleau-Ponty, Maurice (1908–61): French philosopher in whose **phenomenology** central place is given to the idea of embodiment. Merleau-Ponty opposed 'objectivism' unable to give explanations of many disorders of **perception** and **action** in mechanistic causal terms (like phantom limb phenomena). And although he radicalised **Husserl**'s view of science (calling it naive and hypocritical in its ignorance of **consciousness**), he also opposed Husserl's reduction of the natural attitude and **Sartre**'s sovereign *pour-soi*. Nature and consciousness are not opposed to each other, and subjects constitute their environments as essentially embodied beings. The proper body (*le corps propre*) with its motor **intentionality**, not the **Cartesian** ego, gives significations to the world. Action and perception are inseparable, and perception is effected by the body not as a mechanical thing but as consciousness of place intimately connected with its capacity for goal-directed movement. In Merleau-Ponty's later work ('ontology of the flesh') this emphasis on our embodied inherence in being leads him to reject even the notion of intentionality which presupposes a distinction between the subject and the object.

Further reading: Merleau-Ponty [1945] (1962)

Methodological Behaviourism (psychological, empirical behaviourism): The psychological theory of **behaviourism** originated in 1913 from American psychologist John Broadus Watson (1878–1958) and actively advocated by his student Burrhus Frederic Skinner (1904–90). Reacting against the subjectivity of **introspective psychology** and impressed by the work of Russian physiologist Ivan Pavlov (1849–1936) on classical conditioning and associative **learning** in animals, they argued for scientific psychology as the experimental study of observable and measurable behavioural responses to external stimuli. They made laboratory experimentation the main psychological method and resisted **dualism** by closing the gap between humans and 'brutes'. They extended the notion of conditioning to *operant conditioning* whereby an animal learns to do something to achieve some result, and argued that prediction and control of behaviour can be achieved through the discovery of stimuli–response association laws without postulating any changes in animals' knowledge or expectations. Watson later defended **eliminativism** about introspectible states calling the belief in **consciousness** a superstition, whereas Skinner argued for *radical behaviourism* which views all 'private events' as forms of behaviour (**perception** and **introspection** become, respectively, learned responses to environmental reinforcements and one's own observed behaviour). Skinner also extended the paradigm of learning and reinforcement to human language learning. In the 1960s behaviourism began to wane due to **Chomsky's poverty of stimulus argument** and the emerging **computational theory of mind** which made it clear that similar observable behaviour can be generated by systems with different internal structures. **Cognitive ethology** recently became the leading approach to **animal cognition** but behaviourist methodology is preserved in 'behaviour analysis' which sees advantages in approaching the mind as if it were a black box.

Further reading: Watson (1925)

Methodological Solipsism see **Internalism**

Mill, James (1773–1836): Scottish philosopher, father of John Stuart **Mill**. He was a major proponent of **associationism**, and the idea that people can learn to associate personal pleasures with the benefit of others was connected with his moral and political utilitarianism.

Mill, John Stuart (1806–73): British philosopher, a major proponent of **naturalism** in **epistemology**. Mill introduced the notion of **natural kind** and countered **Hume's scepticism** by formulating principles of induction (Mill's methods) pertaining to the discovery of **causal laws**. He also developed early versions of **phenomenalism** and **emergentism**. Distinguishing between denotation (reference) and connotation (sense), between general and **singular** terms, Mill influenced **Frege** (who rejected his **empiricism**) and, holding that proper names have denotation but no connotation, anticipated the **causal theory of reference**.

Further reading: Mill [1843] (2000)

Millikan, Ruth Garrett (b.1933): American philosopher, one of the originators of the **teleological theory of content**. Millikan introduced the notion of 'direct proper function' for biological items, which refers to the function items of a certain type have because its performance by organisms' ancestors contributed to their survival. With respect to the functional **indeterminacy** problem, she argues that one should consider not only mechanisms producing **representations**, but also the 'consumers' of representations, because the purpose of representing is to have an effect on those devices that can put representations to use (a benefit-based theory).

Further reading: Millikan (1984, 2000)

Mind: that which encompasses the full range of mental phenomena: awareness, perception, thought, memory, attention, volition, emotions and feelings. In **modern philosophy** it became identified with **consciousness**, our soul or **self**, the seat of reason and free **will**. In the twentieth century, due to **Freud's** influence and the decline of **Cartesian** substance **dualism**, the connection between mind and consciousness was weakened, becoming severed in **functionalism**. More recently, as a reaction against the emphasis on the **cognitive** mind, the problem of consciousness became prominent in analytical **philosophy of mind**.

Mind–Body Problem: the problem of explaining the place of the **mind** in the physical world, its relationship with the body/**brain**, and the possibility of their interaction or **mental causation**. Solutions to it are provided by: substance and attribute **dualism** (including **interactionism, occasionalism** and **parallelism**), **materialism** (**physicalism**), idealism, panpsychism, neutral monism, epiphenomenalism, emergentism, behaviourism, functionalism and eliminative materialism.

Mirror Neurons: a group of **neurons** in the premotor cortex which become activated both when one is performing a certain task and when one is watching somebody else perform the same task.

Misrepresentation, Problem of (the problem of error): any representing system must be capable of misrepresentation. Your thought of a cat may be caused by something other than a cat (a small dog on a dark night). But your **representation** CAT applies only to cats. The problem for **naturalised semantics** is to explain in non-**intentional** terms how this is possible.

Modal Argument against Physicalism see **Kripke, Saul A.**

Modern Philosophy: began with the rise of modern science in the seventeenth century and continues to set issues for contemporary **philosophy of mind**. Modern philosophy begins with realising that qualities of sense experience are not necessarily qualities of the external world and thus puts **epistemology** at the centre of its psychological concerns, all initiated by **Descartes**. The first issue is the **mind–body problem** stemming from Descartes' substance **dualism**. (**Aristotle**'s view of substances as **universals** transformed by **medieval philosophy**'s view of God as the only substance results in modern philosophy's view of substance as the essence of a kind's existence.) Descartes' **interactionism** puzzled subsequent philosophers who argued that it is impossible for two independent substances to enter into causal interactions (the **interaction problem**). The search for new solutions led to **occasionalism, parallelism, panpsychism, idealism** and infrequent **materialism** (**Hobbes, La Mettrie**). The second problem concerns the relation between **ideas** with which the **mind** operates in thought and that which they are ideas of (**representationalism**), and the origins of the structure of experience and **knowledge** (**rationalism** and **empiricism**). The third problem concerns the relationship between reason and **passions** and the role of the **will**. The end of 'early modern philosophy' came with **Kant** who gave a new expression to these concerns.

Modes of Presentation (MOPs): different ways of conceiving of the same thing. The notion was introduced by **Frege** to account for differences in informational **content** between statements containing coreferential expressions (knowing that my native city is St Petersburg, you may not know that so is Leningrad). For Frege, MOPs are abstract entities that can be grasped by the **mind,** but proponents of **externalism** and Russellian content can view them as psychologically possible ways of thinking about or representing real-world objects and properties.

Modularity: the thesis advanced by **Fodor** that the **mind** contains a number of specialised **information**-processing subsystems or computational mechanisms (*modules*) which encompass the sensory modalities and the language parser (the periphery input systems). The modules are characterised by (1) *domain specificity* (the detection of the melodic structure of acoustic arrays is specific to hearing but not **vision**); (2) mandatory operation (people automatically understand utterances in their native language and do not know what their language 'sounds like' to foreigners); (3) limited central access to **representations** computed by them (having processed an utterance people usually cannot recall the details of syntax, for example whether it was in the active or the passive voice); (4) fast operation; (5) *informational encapsulation* (a module can access only a limited amount of information, that is why some **illusions** persist even when we know that they are illusions); (6) shallow outputs; (7) fixed neural architecture; (8) specific breakdown patterns; (9) characteristic developmental course. In contrast to the modules, the central systems of reasoning which serve philosophical, scientific and much everyday thinking are global, domain-general, **holistic** (or 'Quinean') and isotropic (anything can become relevant to belief formation and revision, which is especially clear in our use of analogies). The thesis proved very influential, but it remains debated whether the modules are mutually impenetrable (some experiments show that auditory information may alter visual **perception**) and *cognitively impenetrable* (is what one sees or hears completely unaffected by what one believes?). Thus, Paul Churchland argues for the theory-ladenness (**plasticity**) of perception, the view that one's theoretical knowledge affects one's perception (think of looking into a microscope). Fodor's notion of modularity can also be distinguished from '**Chomsky**'s modularity' and there is a question whether all of the above characteristics are necessary for modularity (see also **frame problem, massive modularity**).

Further reading: Fodor (1983)

Molecularism: the view that the **content** of a **concept** is determined by its inferential relations with *some* other concepts. It is particularly associated with Christopher Peacocke's version of **functional role semantics**. Peacocke holds that content-constitutive inferences are primitively compelling (someone who has the concept of triangle finds the judgement that triangles have sides primitively compelling). However, spelling this out requires the discredited analytic–synthetic distinction.

Further reading: Peacocke (1992)

Molyneux Problem: was formulated by the Irish surgeon William Molyneux in a letter to **Locke**: would an individual born blind and familiar through touch with the feel of a cube and a sphere made from the same material be able to distinguish which was which visually, without first touching them, if suddenly given sight as an adult? Locke's and **Berkeley**'s answer was no because they believed that **vision** was phenomenally two-dimensional and one learnt about the third dimension through touch. Today, the question does not make sense without further qualification, although most newly sighted individuals either immediately have three-dimensional vision or do not improve with time.

Further reading: Smith (2000)

Monism: the view that there is only one kind of thing underlying all reality. It encompasses **materialism** and **idealism** and is opposed to **dualism**.

Moods: background **phenomenal** states like feeling cheerful, sad, depressed or euphoric which form part of our normal conscious experience (**unity of consciousness**). There is some uncertainty as to whether certain states should be viewed as moods or **emotions,** but the tendency is to distinguish moods by their longer duration and the lack of directedness at specific objects.

Multiple Personalities: the apparent existence of two or more different **persons** or **personalities** in people with multiple personality/dissociative identity disorder. Its main symptom is the lack of personal **memories** extending beyond ordinary forgetfulness. Such people have difficulty forming a stable **self**-conception, but their **unity of consciousness** is intact relative to each 'personality'. If real, which is questioned by some researchers, the disorder poses questions about synchronic **personal identity**.

Multiple Realisability: the thesis that a higher-order functional property may be realised in a variety of distinct physical systems. Thus the property of being an ashtray is independent of the materials ashtrays may be made of. Similarly, any **mental property** (for instance, **pain**) may be realised in physical systems different from our **brains**. This idea was used by **Putnam** in the formulation of **machine functionalism** opposing the **identity theory** which seems to deny mental properties to non-humans (do molluscs feel pain? non-human primates? future robots?). It was taken up by Ned Block and Jerry **Fodor** who noted additional problems posed by neural **plasticity** and convergent **evolution** (though later multiple realisability was turned against **functionalism** in **absent** *qualia* and **Chinese room** arguments). It was then elaborated in Fodor's **special sciences** argument, which distinguished between multiple mental realisability in different kinds of organisms and multiple mental realisability within an individual at different times due to neural plasticity. However, proponents of **reductive physicalism** may argue that multiple realisability is not as radical as it may seem. The extent of neural plasticity is not well understood, and if one leaves aside extraterrestrial creatures and future robots, one has to make sense of some empirical findings. Thus, although the eye evolved several times in unrelated species, its expression was linked to the same genes. Similarly, the same molecular mechanisms (calcium ions) may subserve **cognitive** functions across species. Proponents of **non-reductive physicalism** may respond that multiple realisability is true in so far as the **individuation** of relevant lower-level properties depends on recognising the reality of higher-order mental properties.

Further reading: Block and Fodor (1980)

Myth of the Given: Wilfrid **Sellars'** term for the view that sense experience gives us secure foundations for **knowledge** (foundationalism). Sellars rejected it arguing that experience gets conceptualised by reason and these conceptualisations may be mistaken.

Nagelian Reduction: the first formulation of **intertheoretic reduction** proposed within the framework of **logical positivism** by Ernest Nagel (1901–85). According to it, a higher-level theory (HT) can be reduced to a lower-level theory (LT) if the laws of the former can be logically derived from the laws of the latter via so-called *bridge laws* (bridging principles) which establish empirical type-type biconditional correlations between elements of the two theories ($F_{HT} \longleftrightarrow G_{LT}$). The idea influenced many proponents of the **identity theory** (though not its originators), but later lost its appeal because of **multiple realisability** arguments and the fear (prompting **eliminative materialism**) that it implies not only that mental phenomena

have physical properties but also that physical processes
have mental properties. However, some philosophers argue that it requires only one-way conditionals formulating sufficient conditions at the lower level. Alternatively,
its symmetry may be understood as preserving the dis-
tinctiveness of higher-level phenomena (bridge laws may
be understood as establishing not identities but **nomic** co-
extensiveness of distinct properties).

Further reading: Nagel (1961)

Naive Realism see **Direct Realism**

Narrow Content (cognitive or Fregean epistemic content):
the **content** that **intentional states** (beliefs, desires, etc.)
have intrinsically, independently of an individual's external environment. It is the kind of content that is apparently shared by Oscar and Twin-Oscar in **Putnam's**
Twin-Earth scenario. Proponents of **internalism** hold that
it is more psychologically fundamental than **broad content** because it determines individuals' reasoning and supervenes on their neurophysiology. Many internalists accepted Putnam's argument that only broad contents are
truth-conditional and proposed different ways of isolating narrow contents, viewing them as functions from
contexts to broad contents (early **Fodor**), conceptual
roles (**functional role semantics**), diagonal propositions
(Stalnaker, **Lewis**), or sets of maximal epistemic possibilities or scenarios that an intentional state is compatible
with (Chalmers). However, while these approaches may
succeed in saying what narrow content must be, they are
arguably unable to specify narrow contents of particular thoughts in any other way than making them inef-
fable or identifying them with descriptive contents (but
the inadequacy of descriptions motivated the **causal theory of reference** underlying **externalism** in the first place).

Fodor later concluded that narrow content is unnecessary because Twin cases are an exception to psychological generalisations, and in standard cases it must be nomologically possible for individuals to distinguish between two properties of which they may have thoughts. In contrast, Gabriel Segal argues that **cognitive science** requires only narrow content which is itself truth-conditional (*radical internalism*). Segal admits that many **concepts** (like WATER) are innately determined and triggered by the right causal connections to the environment, but argues that their content changes in the course of one's lifetime as their place in one's reasoning changes. The acceptance of Segal's theory, however, depends on how one views the relationship between concepts and **knowledge** and the idea of conceptual change.

Further reading: Segal (2000)

Nativism see **Rationalism**

Natural Kind: a group of entities which belong together because such is the arrangement of things in nature. Natural kinds are thus scientific or **nomic** kinds which group causally homogeneous (uniform) instances and in terms of which one may formulate **causal laws** and explanations. To decide whether a term designates a natural kind (is a *natural kind predicate*), one can check whether it passes the *projectibility* test. To be projectible, a predicate must provide grounds for induction to allow one to predict the **essential properties** of future instances on the basis of past instances. Thus jade had been thought to be a natural kind until it was discovered that it is really two minerals with different molecular structures – jadeite and nephrite. So because of its disjunctive nature, jade cannot be a natural kind. The notion of natural kind is important to metaphysical **essentialism** and the debate between

non-reductive and **reductive physicalism**. The difficulty with understanding biological species in terms of hidden internal structure led some philosophers of biology to reject essentialism or view species as individuals, whereas others argue that science should include historical kinds (those whose essence depends on having a certain causal history), the view that supports **externalism**.

Naturalism: the view that the mental forms part of the natural order and that its explanation must be continuous with explanations in natural sciences (be compatible with **physicalism**).

   Further reading: Papineau (1993)

Naturalised Semantics: the approach to explaining **intentionality** and mental **content** in naturalistic terms, without appeal to semantic notions like 'believe', 'mean', 'refer', 'be about', 'be true'. Because intentional properties cannot be the fundamental features of reality, it must be shown how physical systems can have **intentional states**. It includes the **informational** and **teleological theory of content**. Philosophers sceptical of the naturalising project argue that the 'intentional idiom' is irreducible (because of the **normativity, rationality** and **holism** of the mental) or believe that such understanding is cognitively closed to us.

Neo-Darwinism see **Adaptationism**

Neural Constructivism: the view, supportive of **connectionism** (the PDP version), that neural mechanisms of **cognitive** development are those of constructive **learning**: the representational complexity of the cortex, initially free of domain-specific structure, is built by the environment operating on it. The view, however, ignores the fact that cortical development is inseparable from the development of subcortical input systems (a mole raised in the same environment as a rat will not develop cortical structures for visual processing) and it is not clear how sensory input itself could generate an increase in representational power.

Further reading: Quartz and Sejnowsky (1997)

Neural Darwinism (selectionism): the view that the main neural mechanism of cognitive development is the execution of a genetically coded maturational programme. That is, the establishment of specialised neural circuits (for example, for processing visual **information**) is itself independent of the environmental input, and the impact of the environment consists in the selective elimination or 'pruning' of such specialised circuits whose numbers are initially redundant. It is supported by the fact that in early development exuberant dendritic growth ('arborisation') is followed by a sharp decrease in synaptic density within a short period of time. The view, however, posits **innate** connectivity patterns, not innate representational **content**.

Further reading: Edelman (1987)

Neural Networks see **Connectionism**

Neurons: cells in the nervous system subserving its **information**-processing functions (more numerous *glial cells* are thought to have supporting functions). Neurons consist of the cell body (*soma*), the output fibre (*axon*) and input fibres (*dendrites*). The point at which the axon terminal contacts other neurons' dendrites and somata is the *synapse*. Information between neurons is communicated by means of *synaptic transmission*: a neuron becomes active ('fires') and sends its electrochemical signal to other neurons with which it is connected. These details are captured in **connectionism,** but the action potential is 'all-or-none', and information-coding is realised by neurons' differential spatiotemporal firing patterns ('spikes', the amplitude and frequency of generated impulses, and variation in time intervals between them) followed by neurotransmitter release at the synapse. After the work of **Hebb** and others, it is believed that the **brain's representations** of properties are stored in the connectivity patterns of distributed neuronal groups. It is also possible that specialised neuronal groups selectively code for specific features. Following Torsten Wiesel and David Hubel's discovery of orientation-selective neurons in striate visual cortex ('edge-detection cells'), several investigations suggested the existence of specialised neurons processing information about faces ('grandmother cells'). But selective cells were also shown to respond to a range of features and individual neurons may participate in coding for several properties. The problem is to understand how representation of determinate properties can be maintained by units with multiple-property sensitivity (the question of the brain's topology). The issue of specialised neuronal representation is central to debates about neural **plasticity** and neural mechanisms of **cognitive** development (**neural constructivism** *versus* **neural Darwinism**).

Further reading: Bear et al. (2001)

Neurophilosophy: an approach to the **mind/brain** defended by Paul and Patricia Churchland. According to it, facts discovered by **neuroscience** are immediately relevant to **philosophy of mind**. This, however, takes the form of a continued attack on **folk psychology**, initiated by **eliminative materialism**, combined with a philosophical apology of **connectionism** (the PDP version). Connectionism is said to capture principles of **representation** in biological systems (activity vectors) that are incompatible with discrete representational states of the **language of thought** (LOT) and the logico-semantic inferences of the **computational theory of mind**. The main argument in favour of connectionist representation in the brain is *graceful degradation* of **cognitive** functions. While damage to a symbolic system (removal of a symbol or rule) often results in a sharp decline in its performance, distributed representations exhibit greater **plasticity** so that representations become blurred rather than disappear completely and partial retrieval remains possible. This pattern is indeed characteristic of some cognitive deficits, but other deficits arguably follow the pattern of representational disruption in symbolic systems (the **Williams syndrome**, severe category-specific semantic impairments: selective loss of **concepts** for animals, tools or numbers). Besides, given neurophilosophers' view that today's science may not be the science of the future, an a priori conclusion that the brain cannot support the language of thought seems unwarranted.

Further reading: Churchland (1986), Churchland (1995)

Neuroscience: the study of the nervous system, especially the **brain,** by invasive (destruction of brain areas, gene 'knockout' in non-human animals, electrode recording of neuronal firing) and non-invasive scanning methods like functional magnetic resonance imaging (fMRI) and positron emission tomography (PET). Neuroscience is often contrasted with **cognitive science** because it does not separate **mind** and brain, but many neuroscientific investigations (for example, lesion studies) require the use of **mental concepts** (*neuropsychology, cognitive neuroscience*).

Further reading: Bear et al. (2001)

Neutral Monism: the view that the primal stuff of reality is neither mental nor physical. It was held by Ernest Mach, **James** and **Russell** (briefly). The primal stuff (identified with the stream of sensible qualities or James's 'pure experience') is mental only when taken in some arrangements or contexts of associated qualities (thus, neutral monism makes **consciousness** non-substantial). The view may be hard to distinguish from **panpsychism** or attribute **dualism**.

New Wave Materialism see **Identity Theory**

New Wave Reductionism: the approach identifying **mental states** with **brain** states developed by John Bickle. Bickle rejects **Nagelian reduction** which retains all properties of the reduced theory and elaborates on Clifford Hooker's view that **intertheoretic reduction** involves a continuum of 'smooth', 'revisionary' and 'bumpy' reductions (Thomas Kuhn's idea of discontinuous scientific development). Bickle proposes the following scheme: for the theory to be reduced (TR, **folk psychology**) one constructs its image model (TR*) which uses only those terms that are available in the base theory (TB, **neuroscience**). TR* (psychology formulated in neuroscientific terms) derived from TB (neuroscience) will be only partly isomorphic with TR (folk psychology). The idea is thus that the functional organisation of **cognition** and the notion of **representation** will be preserved, but specific mental states postulated by folk psychology (and **language of thought**) will be eliminated. Following Robert McCauley one may object that Bickle conflates *intralevel* and *interlevel* reduction: whereas the former involves elimination (like the elimination of phlogiston from chemistry), the latter does not (quantum mechanics eliminated neither macrophysical objects nor their physics). The approach thus runs against the problem of **mental concepts** that arises for **eliminative materialism.**

Further reading: Bickle (1998)

Nomic: (1) capable of being subsumed under **causal laws;** (2) lawlike.

Nomological: relating to the laws of nature. Nomological possibility is consistency with **causal laws** of the actual world.

Nomological Danglers: Herbert Feigl's term for the irreducible mental properties of **dualism** which dangle from the **nomological** net of physical sciences, being unnecessary and implausible.

Further reading: Feigl (1958)

Non-conceptual Content: the **content** of **mental states** not represented with the help of **concepts** (the notion was introduced by Evans to explain the possibility of **demonstrative content**). Perceptual experience obviously has propositional content (it represents the world as being a certain way), but perceptual **representation** seems distinct from representation in belief: (1) it is informationally rich: as the subject cannot deploy concepts for every object and property represented in **perception**, one may perceive something without forming concepts (**Dretske**); (2) it is analogue: unlike belief it carries with it extra **information** and is continuously variable (we perceive something as varying in brightness without detecting discrete states – earlier Dretske; but note that analogue representation can be reproduced digitally, so this may be a question of availability to **consciousness**); (3) it is more finely grained because we perceive more than we have concepts for (like various colours and shapes – Christopher Peacocke). Peacocke developed an account of non-conceptual *scenario content* to explain how organisms represent in experience spatial properties of their environments relative to themselves ('to the left') without having the corresponding concepts. (In Peacocke's **molecularism** and Bermúdez's theory of non-conceptual **self-consciousness** concepts are linguistic, judgement-dependent, entities.) Most proponents of **representationalism about consciousness** also argue for the non-conceptual content of experience as that which alone distinguishes perceptual representation from belief. The exact understanding of the notion, however, depends on how one understands concepts and the relation between perceptual discrimination and merely sensory experience.

Further reading: Gunther (2003)

Non-reductive Physicalism: the view that **mental properties** are irreducible to physical properties, that the mental qua mental matters in causing behaviour (that it is your belief that it is raining together with your desire not to get wet that makes you take an umbrella with you). The essential point is commitment to **multiple realisability** or the **supervenience** thesis: physical indistinguishability implies mental indistinguishability, but mental indistinguishability does not imply physical indistinguishability. However, there arises the problem of **mental causation**: how can mental properties qua mental cause behaviour? Responses to the problem include: (1) **overdetermination**; (2) **counterfactual causation**; (3) pragmatic theories; (4) the layered view of the world (see also **emergentism**). Pragmatic theories distinguish between causal efficacy and causal relevance or suitability for causal explanations given our **cognitive** limitations. But the solution is problematic because, arguably, acceptable explanation must address the issue of causation. According to the many layers view, reality itself has many levels of organisation, and mental properties are genuine causal properties (mental **realism** found, for instance, in **Fodor's** argument from **causal laws**). However, this raises the question of how higher-order properties could have causal powers beyond those of their physical realisers and the issue of their mind-dependence: in what sense do **special sciences'** entities exist for creatures incapable of representing them? The **mind–body problem** thus becomes related to the problem of **intentionality**.

Further reading: Heil and Mele (1993)

Normativity: sensitivity to norms, to what is acceptable and what is not. In our everyday explanation of behaviour (**folk psychology**) we implicitly presuppose norms governing reasoning and **action** of rational beings. The normativity of our **mental concepts** poses problems for reductive and eliminative explanations of mentality because science is descriptive, not prescriptive, and one cannot derive 'ought' from 'is' (this is questioned today by **teleological** approaches).

Occasionalism: the view that all sequences of events conceivable of as cause and effect are occasioned by God, to whom alone causal powers must be ascribed. Occasionalism arose in Islamic thought in the ninth century, becoming especially prominent in the philosophy of Abu Hamid Muhammad Al-Ghazali (1059–1111). In **modern philosophy** it was held by Johannes Clauberg, Arnold Geulinex, Louis de la Forge and Nicolas **Malebranche.** Occasionalism may be best understood in the context of the theory of **ideas** which views **causal laws** (including general laws of the union of soul and body) as propositions in the mind of God whose efficacy depends on being constantly entertained by Him (the doctrine of continuous creation).

Occurrent: occurrent **mental states** are those that: (1) occur within a **cognitive** system at some specific moment of time; (2) subjects are aware of being in.

Ockham's Razor see **Universals**

Ontology: (1) a complete collection of entities which really exist; (2) the study of what exists.

Other Minds: the problem of knowing that other people have **minds** and avoiding **solipsism** that arises for the **Cartesian** view according to which we have **privileged access** to our own **mental states** and infallible **self-knowledge**, but only indirect **knowledge** of others' minds. The standard response is that having mental states is the best explanation we have of our behaviour, and we conclude that others have minds by noticing their similarity to us and observing their behaviour (the 'argument from analogy' associated with J. S. **Mill**). **Behaviourism** and **interpretivism** oppose the Cartesian view holding that knowledge of our own minds depends on our being members of our linguistic communities. **Sartre** also opposed this view arguing that we have immediate awareness of others' minds, and **Searle** questions **functionalism** on the grounds that our knowledge of ourselves involves knowing that we have the right physiology. Today the issue is debated by **theory theory** and **simulation theory**.
    Further reading: Avramides (2001)

Overdetermination: the view that an event can have two independent causes (two bullets causing the same death) intended to explain the possibility of downward **mental**

causation. However, it violates the **causal closure of the physical.**

Pain: an unpleasant **sensation** normally arising from the application of noxious stimuli to a group of sensory **neurons** with peripheral terminals (primary afferent nociceptors, types Aδ and C). Pain has been the most discussed example in the context of the **mind–body problem** since **behaviourism**. **Kripke's** argument that pain and C-fibres firing are related only contingently questioned the **identity theory**. Because damage to the 'pain pathway' (spinal cord, thalamus, cortex) will prevent cortically based pain experience, this is true, but pain researchers do not agree that pain cannot be identified with any physical property. The **reductive–non-reductive physicalism** debate posed other important questions: is there such a thing as pain in general? do all pain-feeling organisms experience the same pain and how can one determine what organisms are capable of feeling pain? Viewing pain as a single property prevents its **reduction** (for example, different molecular mechanisms are implicated in different kinds of headaches). However, there is also a strong intuition that our **mental concept** of pain picks out a single property. **Functionalism** captures this intuition, but cannot explain pain's **phenomenal** feel (pain does not disturb frontal lobotomy patients; 'phantom limb' pains are apparently non-functional). Finally, whereas **epiphenomenalism** about pain is probably true (pain does not cause withdrawal; but not if quantum information travels back in time, as holds Stuart Hameroff), there is also an issue of **mental causation** and placebo effects (how do beliefs that some stuff will work cause pain to go away?).

Panpsychism: the view that all constituents of reality have some mental properties. Different versions of panpsychism have been entertained throughout the history of philosophy and are found in **Spinoza, Leibniz** (on some interpretations), Schelling, Schopenhauer, **Wundt, James, Peirce** and Whitehead. Panpsychism, including its recent versions, is motivated by the idea that otherwise it would be impossible to explain why complex entities have **(phenomenal) consciousness** (the problem of establishing when, where and how consciousness emerges).

Further reading: Rosenberg (2004)

Parallel Distributed Processing see **Connectionism**

Parallelism (psychophysical parallelism): the view that mental and physical phenomena have parallel existence with no causal interaction between them. Developed by **Spinoza** and **Leibniz** in response to the **interaction problem**, it was often held in conjunction with **panpsychism.**

Passions: an umbrella term for **emotions** and desires viewed as passive, irrational and having to be controlled by the **will.** This view is often associated with **modern philosophy** before **Hume.** However, **Descartes** held that passions, disciplined by reason, contribute to our practical and theoretical **rationality**, that wonder is necessary to motivate the soul toward the search of truth, that mental contentment may serve as evidence that a truth has been attained.

Peirce, Charles Sanders (1839–1914): American philosopher, the founder of **pragmatism**. Peirce introduced the notion of **abduction** and the distinction between signs (icons) and symbols used in the discussion of the **evolution** of animal communication and human language (but Peirce viewed symbols as artificial signs). He defended **panpsychism,**

holding that the materialist view of the **mind** as a mechanism capable of feeling is not a clear hypothesis.

Further reading: Peirce (1992)

Perception: the process by which features of external reality are detected in the modalities of **vision**, audition, touch (haptic modality), olfaction (smell) and gustation (taste), encoded in the **brain**, integrated into **representations** of objects and properties and, frequently, presented to individual awareness in conscious experience. Perception is distinguished from both **sensation** and **cognition**, and the issues it raises lie on the intersection of **epistemology** and the problem of **consciousness**. In having perceptual experiences (seeing a ginger cat, hearing a door bang) we seem to be immediately aware of a mind-independent reality with its spatial structure and discrete material objects. But our perceptual experiences are not always *veridical* (accurate), so **illusion**, **hallucination** and **dreaming** pose the question of whether the immediate *objects* of perception are outside or inside the **mind**. There are also issues concerning the relation between perception and **knowledge** of the world, the **content** and the **phenomenal** character (*qualia*) of perceptual experience. **Representationalism**, the leading theory of perception, is contrasted with the **sense-datum theory, adverbialism, idealism, phenomenalism, direct perception** theories and **disjunctivism**. The issue of **modularity** versus theory-ladenness of perception and the relation between perception and **categorisation** are also subject to debates.

Further reading: Smith (2002); Gendler Szabo and Hawthorne (2006)

Person: being a person is usually identified with having continuous identity with oneself which requires certain mental features like **consciousness**, conscious **memory**, self-consciousness, capacity for **rationality**, free **agency**, morality and meaningful life. Traditionally, being a person was understood as having an immutable immaterial soul maintaining its identity over a person's life and perhaps thereafter. This view is preserved in today's infrequent substance **dualism** originating in **Descartes'** notion of the **self**. Its proponents (Roderick Chisholm, Geoffrey Mandell, Richard Swinburne, John Foster) hold that, whereas we can speak of partial identity for material things, the notions of partial identity and survival for **minds** or souls are conceptually incoherent because a person's conscious states either belong to them or not and one cannot analyse personhood in terms of body and **brain** parts (we can imagine ourselves acquiring new bodies). But dualism is unconvincing to most philosophers, and new principles of **individuation** for persons must be found, as the notion has implications for assigning moral responsibility and making correct decisions about people in a persistent vegetative state, animals and embryos. This may require the notion of degrees of personhood.

Further reading: Foster (1996); Perring (1997)

Personal Identity: we have an intuition of being the same **person** over the course of our lives. The problem of personal identity is to find the necessary and sufficient conditions for someone X to survive changes or remain the same entity at different times (what makes one be the same thing at age 5, 25, 35, etc.?) This is the issue of one's *persistence* in time (diachronic identity) which presupposes absolute numeric **identity** for persons. The discussion was spurred by research on **split-brains** and involves considering the implications of **brain** *transplantation* (when your brain is transplanted into a different body, do you go with the brain or stay with the old body?) and *fission* (when your cerebral hemispheres are transplanted into different bodies, where do you go?) **thought experiments**. The most widespread approach, associated with **Locke**, views personal identity in terms of psychological continuity in conscious **memory** and causal dependence between one's mental features (Thomas Nagel, Harold Noonan, Derek Parfit, Sydney Shoemaker). But as it seems to deny our continuity with embryos and possible future people in a vegetative state, it implies that we are not human animals. It also must admit for fission cases that one could be mentally continuous with two future people. Parfit argues that it is not identity that matters but whether there will be someone mentally continuous with one in the future (he defends partial continuity and argues that the 'further fact' view of **dualism** about persons rests on a conceptual mistake). Contrasted with the psychological approach is *animalism* (the somatic approach) which sees personal identity as a matter of brute physical continuity (David Wiggins, Paul Snowdon, Eric Olson), but transplantation cases pose a problem for it.

Further reading: Parfit (1984); Olson (1997)

Personality (character): the sum of an individual's stable psychological traits analysed along five dimensions: introverted–extroverted, neurotic–stable, incurious–open to experience, agreeable–antagonistic, conscientious–undirected. Philosophical questions include: the relation between being a **person** and having a unique personality; qualitative **personal identity** over time; the determination of one's **actions** by one's personality; and the interaction between genes, experience and social factors in shaping personality.

Phenomenal: appearing to an individual in a certain way. Phenomenal states are **mental states** with *qualia* (confusingly, they are sometimes distinguished from phenomenally

conscious states or states available to subjective awareness but without associated 'feels', for example, beliefs).

Phenomenal Concepts: concepts we have of our sensory
states (feeling **pain**, experiencing a **colour** sensation).
Several philosophers (Brian Loar, Brian McLaughlin,
Christopher Hill, David Papineau, Michael Tye) hold
that understanding their nature gives the **identity theory** an argument against **Kripke's** problem, **zombies** and
the **knowledge argument**. The idea is that the identity of
mental states with brain states, though necessary a posteriori, appears to be contingent because of the special nature of phenomenal **concepts**, importantly different from
physical-functional or theoretical concepts. Phenomenal
concepts are direct recognitional concepts whose possession is linked with having the right kind of experience
and the capacity to reidentify its instances in **introspection**
and **imagination**. The existence of different concepts does
not imply the existence of different properties. Phenomenal concepts refer directly to the same properties that
are referred to by the corresponding physical-functional
concepts, and the appearance of contingency is due to
their distinctive role in our **cognitive** life. David Chalmers
objects that this strategy assumes rather than explains
identity and leaves unanswered the question of why two
distinct concepts should pick out the same property (it
explains why zombies are conceivable, but does not explain why, despite that, they are impossible).
Further reading: Loar (1997); Chalmers (1999);
Papineau (2002)

Phenomenal Consciousness: experience with its particular
subjective feel. **Phenomenal** states possess qualitative features (*qualia*), and if there is something that an experience

feels like to you, then you are phenomenally conscious of it. Phenomenal consciousness poses problems for both **physicalism** and **functionalism** because it is hard to understand how and why **brain** states or functional states should give rise to *qualia*, to the **what-it's-like** character of subjective experience (David Chalmers called this the Hard Problem of Consciousness). Why should **colour** experiences or **emotions** feel a certain way to us? Why could there not be beings just like us but having no phenomenal consciousness (**zombies**)? Is phenomenal consciousness **epiphenomenal**? **Consciousness** is known to us only through **introspection**. This creates a clash between the first-person and the third-person (scientific) perspectives and suggests that in trying to explain consciousness we may be faced with the **explanatory gap**. In a broader sense, as understood in **phenomenology**, phenomenal consciousness is not limited to the qualitative character of experience but encompasses its organisation as a whole.

Further reading: Chalmers (1996)

Phenomenal Realism see **Realism**

Phenomenalism: an epistemological theory of **perception** held by J. S. **Mill, Russell** and some philosophers of **logical positivism** (Ayer, **Carnap**). It views objects of perception as **sense-data** providing the foundation of all **knowledge**, and material objects as 'permanent possibilities of **sensation**' (Mill). For Russell, physical objects were logical constructions out of sensations (sensibilia) immediately given in perceptual experience (logical atomism). In logical positivism it turned into a programme of translating empirical statements into statements about the **phenomenal**. The project was not completed as it proved impossible to explain orderly occurrences of phenomenal properties in experience without reference to public objects.

Further reading: Russell (1956)

Phenomenological Fallacy: the fallacy of inferring from appearance to existence. **Place** used the expression for the mistake of supposing that when people describe their experiences (that something looks green to them), they describe properties of some internal **mental objects** (of something green existing in the **mind**).

Phenomenology: (1) the **phenomenal** character of experience (*qualia*); (2) the tradition of **philosophy of mind** developed by Edmund **Husserl**, Martin Heidegger, Jean-Paul **Sartre** and Maurice **Merleau-Ponty** as the study of **consciousness** from the first-person perspective intended to uncover in experience those components that account for its **intentionality.**

Philosophy of Mind: studies the nature of mental phenomena (thought, belief, desire, sensation, perception, volition, emotion, etc.). Its main issues are the **mind–body problem** and **intentionality (content).** The problem of intentionality marked the divergence between analytical and continental traditions (**phenomenology**). Phenomenology holds that the essence of **mind** is **consciousness** and emphasises the first-person perspective. Analytical tradition, shaped by **Frege** and **Russell**, emphasises the importance of conceptual analysis of mental terms and aims to make mentality amenable to scientific (third-person) investigation. With the recent resurgence of interest in the problem of consciousness, the relation between intentionality and consciousness and their evolutionary emergence are becoming the central issue of today's philosophy of mind.

Physical Realisation Principle: the principle, accepted by proponents of **non-reductive physicalism,** that if any x has a mental property M, there is a physical property P such that x has P and, necessarily, anything that has P has M (and P realises M).

Physical Stance see **Intentional Stance**

Physicalism (Materialism): the view that everything in the universe is physical or not requiring for its existence anything over and above entities and processes recognised by the physical sciences (physics, but also chemistry and biology). It is useful to distinguish between (1) *token* and *type* physicalism, (2) *reductive* and *non-reductive* physicalism and (3) *a priori* and *a posteriori* physicalism. *Token physicalism* holds that every mental event (like having a **pain**) is identical with some physical event, whereas *type physicalism* holds that every type of mental event, or every **mental property**, is identical with some physical property (being in a neural state of certain type). Token physicalism is compatible with attribute **dualism** and must be augmented with the idea of **supervenience** or the **physical realisation principle,** as physicalism is opposed to dualism. This gives us *supervenience physicalism.* Supervenience physicalism (first formulated as **anomalous monism**) is a species of **non-reductive physicalism,** whereas type physicalism (first formulated as the **identity theory**) is a species of **reductive physicalism.** *A priori physicalism* and *a posteriori physicalism* are forms of reductive physicalism urging either an a priori (conceptual; **Lewis's** contingent, **Jackson's** necessary) or an a posteriori (empirical; the identity theory) identification of **mental states** with physical states. Finally, note that physicalism encompasses **eliminative materialism** and **functionalism,** and although it is sometimes contrasted with functionalism, in such cases it should be understood as reductive physicalism, since functionalism accepts the core physicalist commitment.

Further reading: Gillett and Loewer (2001)

Place, Ullin T. (1924–2000): British-Australian philosopher, originator of the **identity theory**. Place argued for the constitution of **consciousness** by **brain** processes as a scientific hypothesis. However, he never extended the theory to beliefs and desires, insisting that they, as we do not sense them, should be given a **dispositional** analysis. In later work he developed the idea of two parallel processing systems, the **unconscious** system ('**zombie**-within') and consciousness, whose function is to deal with problematic inputs.

Further reading: Place (1956)

Plasticity (equipotentiality): the capacity of distinct neural structures to subserve identical psychological functions and take on new functions as a result of **learning** or **brain** damage. Proponents of **connectionism, neurophilosophy** and **neural constructivism** argue against **innate** domain-specific representational structures in the **brain**, quoting instances of cortical remapping and tissue relocation, foetal cortical tissue transplantation, rewiring of primary sensory areas (as in Mriganka Sur's experiments when young ferrets' auditory cortex was rewired to process visual information), and resumption of **cognitive** functions in young children following brain lesions (left hemisphere removal). However, other data show that the brain is not totally plastic (early damage to prefrontal areas leads to irrepairable cognitive deficits) and remapping is subject to structural constraints (the primary auditory cortex of rewired ferrets retains connections to other brain areas for hearing and has low resolution visual representation). The existence of neural plasticity and its support of **multiple realisability** raise important issues for empirical research: to what extent are **neurons'** representational properties determined by their functional roles in contrast to their intrinsic properties? what factors (neuroanatomical, neurofunctional, neurophysiological) determine when two distinct neural states belong to the same kind (the problem of **individuation**)?

Plato (*c.* 427–347 BC): ancient Greek philosopher, the major source of philosophical inspiration which brought him the title of *princeps totius philosophiae*, the best of philosophers. From the early dialogues, where Plato introduces the questioning figure of Socrates, particularly interesting is *Meno* with its formulation of the **learning** paradox: one cannot learn something of which one has no prior understanding. In the middle dialogues (*Phaedo, The Republic*) the Socratic method and the search for essences of what is expressed by our **concepts** of justice, virtue or love are replaced with the positive theory of *Forms* or *Ideas*: changeless, independent of things, abstract entities from which things with the same form receive their nature, and of which the highest is that of the Good. The forms can be apprehended by *noesis*, the highest type of **knowledge**, which is the recollection of the acquaintance with the forms that the impersonal, immortal, rational soul (*nous*) contemplated before becoming imprisoned in the body (the theory of *anamnesis*). Plato's eidetic theory (*eidos*, form) is the first account of the world's intelligibility opposing the **scepticism** engendered by the changeability of perceptual experience. It it is also the first formulation of the symbolic character of thought (**representational theory of mind**) and the problem of **universals**. From the late middle dialogues, *Parmenides* presents a critique of the theory of forms later adopted by **Aristotle**, and *Theaetetus* develops the conception of knowledge as justified true belief (albeit this reading of Plato may be questioned).

Further reading: Plato (1989)

Possible Worlds: a technical device for clarifying intuitions about modality (possibility and necessity) and analysing counterfactual **thought and language** (if x had happened, y would have happened). Possible worlds are complete states of affairs which differ from the actual (our) world in some details. They may be understood as alternative scenarios of how things might have been in the actual world (**Kripke**), as elements of the conceptual space (Robert Stalnaker), or as existing just as this world does (**Lewis**'s *modal realism*). In Kripke's modal **logic** propositions must be evaluated as true or false at possible worlds, and a proposition is necessary if it is true at all possible worlds (**Leibniz**'s view). Kripke's notion of necessity is important for discussions of the **mind–body problem** and the issue of whether, apart from **nomological** necessity, one should recognise both metaphysical and conceptual necessity or whether these are the same thing (the **zombies** argument is based on the latter view). Stalnaker's **deflationism** about possible worlds shows how the **informational theory of content** and the view of **propositional attitudes** as relations to propositions (semantically evaluable abstract objects) are made compatible through an analysis of propositions as sets of possible worlds (to have a conception of the world is to locate it in a space of possibilities). Stalnaker's and Lewis's notion of similarity between possible worlds, which allows one to evaluate counterfactual statements as true if they are true at all worlds most similar to ours, is relevant to the idea of **counterfactual causation** and the **externalism–internalism** debate.

Poverty of Stimulus: the argument given by **Chomsky** in his 1959 review of Skinner's *Verbal Behaviour* (1956). Because children receive highly impoverished stimuli from adults (they are not explicitly taught to speak and are seldom corrected) no general **learning** mechanism (imitation, association, reinforcement) can explain how children master linguistic competence at the rates at which they actually master it.

Pragmatism: (1) the view associated with **James, Peirce** and John Dewey that the meaning of a doctrine and its truth must be understood in terms of its practical effects on one's **action** in the world; (2) **Fodor**'s recent term for theories of **concepts** which identify possessing a concept *X* with being able to sort things into *X*s and non-*X*s (Dewey, **behaviourism**, some theories of **categorisation**). This idea underlies the notion of *recognitional (observational)* concepts like RED or APPLE which are thought to be based on discriminatory capacities. But pragmatism is also characteristic of **functional role semantics** which holds that having inferential capacities is constitutive of concept possession. (Pragmatism was anticipated by Thomas Reid who rejected the existence of **ideas** as mental entities but accepted them as acts of thought; see also **Putnam.**) The problem with pragmatism is that such capacities are themselves parasitic on **representation** (one must represent apples to oneself before being able to pile them separately from pears), and that it violates the **compositionality** constraint.

Further reading: Fodor (2003)

Pre-established Harmony see **Leibniz, Gottfried Wilhelm**

Preconscious see **Freud, Sigmund**

Primary and Secondary Qualities: the distinction drawn by **Locke** (still relevant to theories of **perception**) between qualities like size, shape and motion which are objective properties of things or primary qualities (he sometimes adds solidity and texture) and qualities like **colour**, sound, taste and smell which are things' **dispositions** to change sensory states of perceivers and in a sense exist only in individuals' **minds** (secondary or immediate sensory qualities). The main criterion for the distinction is not being tied to one particular sense modality.

Principle of Charity: the principle formulated by **Davidson** that in interpreting other people's behaviour we ascribe to them beliefs and desires they should rationally have in their situation. Because the interpreter must thus presuppose that people's beliefs are mostly true, the principle supports **externalism** and provides an argument against **scepticism**.

Principle of Humanity: the principle that in interpreting other people's behaviour we do not try to maximise the **rationality** and truth of their beliefs as required by the **principle of charity,** but rather invoke considerations of what is sufficiently reasonable for them to believe. The principle is compatible with **internalism.**

Privacy: that feature of the **mind** in virtue of which a subject's thoughts and experiences are accessible only to themselves (**privileged access**).

Private Language Argument see **Wittgenstein, Ludwig**

Privileged Access: the idea, deriving from **Descartes,** that a person has immediate epistemic access to their **mental**

states. Although this view leads to the problem of **other minds,** what sort of privileged access we enjoy remains an important issue in discussions of **consciousness** and **self-knowledge.**

Productivity: the property of **thought and language** whereby an infinite number of thoughts and sentences can be formed on the basis of a finite set of primitive elements and **recursive** syntactic rules.

Proper Function see **Millikan, Ruth Garrett**

Propositional Attitudes: psychological relations of persons to propositions. Propositional attitudes are individuated by their psychological type like thinking, believing, desiring, knowing, doubting, hoping, fearing, etc. (expressed linguistically by a corresponding *psychological or propositional attitude verb*) and the proposition that forms their **content** (expressed linguistically by a 'that'-clause). 'Fears that it will rain', 'hopes that it will rain', 'believes that Edinburgh is in Scotland' and 'believes that Edinburgh is not in Scotland' are different propositional attitudes, the most discussed kind of **intentional states.** One interesting feature of psychological verbs is that they create **intensional** or *referentially opaque* contexts. In extensional or *referentially transparent* contexts one can substitute co-referring expressions for one another without affecting the truth-value of a sentence: 'Mark Twain was a writer' and 'Samuel Clemens was a writer' are both true (*intersubstitutivity salva veritate*). But 'Ann believes that Mark Twain was a writer' and 'Ann believes that Samuel Clemens was a writer' may have different truth-values, for Ann may not know that Samuel Clemens was Mark Twain's real name. This phenomenon, identified by **Frege** and **Russell**, is known as the *failure of substitutivity of co-referential expressions* in contexts created by psychological verbs, and the problem it creates is the *co-reference problem*. Another interesting feature of psychological verbs is that whereas 'Mary hates George' entails that George exists, 'Mary wants to find the Fountain of Youth' does not entail that the Fountain of Youth exists. This is the failure of *existential generalisation* in intensional contexts. However, **knowledge, perception** and remembering ('knows, perceives, remembers that p') constitute an exception because they do entail the existence of objects they are directed at and are called for this reason *factive attitudes*.

Prototype Theory: the most popular theory of **concepts** in **cognitive psychology** according to which concepts are sets of typical features. Prototype theory, motivated by problems with the **definitional theory** and **Wittgenstein**'s notion of family resemblances, was proposed by Eleanor Rosch who noticed striking *prototypicality effects* in people's judgements of category membership. Thus people more readily judge that robins are birds than that penguins are birds and the number of **categorisation** mistakes is related to the typicality of instances (typical birds fly, have feathers, sing, are small, etc.). Rosch also introduced the notion of the *basic level* of categorisation, concepts from which (DOG) are richer in their informational potential, have closer links with **perception** and are acquired before concepts from the subordinate (POODLE) and superordinate (ANIMAL) levels. Rosch's ideas were later developed into a formal theory which views concepts as structured mental **representations** coding for typical properties of objects that these concepts refer to (Edward Smith, James Hampton). Like the definitional theory, it endows concepts with internal structure, but posits *statistical* instead of logical structure. Thus **connectionism** is seen as complementing it. But prototype theory faces the problem of concept shareability (even if people's concepts are not identical but merely similar, one must distinguish in them a common core, which requires viewing some features as identical), **compositionality** (the **content** of PET FISH is not composed from the prototypes of PET and FISH), and the fact that people's **knowledge** of objects is not identical with the concepts they have of them (people do judge penguins to be birds).

Psychoanalysis see **Freud, Sigmund**

Psychofunctionalism see **Machine Functionalism**

Psychological Laws see **Causal Laws**

Psychophysical Laws: laws correlating **brain** properties and **mental properties.** Their existence is debated by different versions of **physicalism.**

Putnam, Hilary (b. 1926): American philosopher, the originator of **machine functionalism** and **externalism.** Although scientific **realism,** realism about the mental and contemporary **functionalism** are all indebted to Putnam (he coined the term 'functionalism'), in the 1980s he became sceptical about the functionalist characterisation of **mental states** thinking that **multiple realisability** applies not only to physical but also to computational states. The problem with functionalism, arising from the **holism** of the mental, lies in its approach to the **individuation** of **intentional states** (saying when an organism has a belief with a certain **content** like 'it is snowing'). To hold that the aim of psychological explanation is to produce a complete functional description of psychological states of an arbitrary organism is a utopia. There is an infinite number of possible interpretations of what an organism believes given a piece of its linguistic and non-linguistic behaviour. And one cannot individuate beliefs by specifying the *totality* of an organism's functional states because of Gödel's incompleteness theorem: the mind cannot survey its own limits. Thus **intentionality** is irreducible and scientific realism (the view that there is one true description of reality) is a myth. This made Putnam a critic of **functional role semantics** and **informational theory of content**. He also rejects **representationalism** about **perception** (in favour of **direct perception**), and sees **cognitive science** as the Cartesian theatre plus **materialism** (but he is also sceptical of **neuroscience**). Concurrently, his positive position was *internal realism*, which was becoming closer and closer to **pragmatism** and epistemological **relativism**.

Further reading: Putnam (1988, 2000)

qua problem: arises for the **causal theory of reference** and the **informational theory of content**. The problem is to explain how we manage to refer to or represent a certain kind of things, say, tigers qua tigers rather than qua animals as the same individual that serves to fix the reference of 'tiger' is both a tiger and an animal.

Further reading: Sterelny (1983)

qualia (singular: *quale*): qualitative or **phenomenal** properties of experience. Seeing red, feeling **pain** or tasting a lemon feel to us a certain way, there is something that it is like for us to have these experiences. It means that these **mental states** have *qualia*. Most philosophers agree that mental states with *qualia* include experiences of **perception** (hearing a loud noise), bodily **sensations** (feeling an itch), felt **emotions** (fear) and **moods** (depression). Galen Strawson argues that thoughts also have *qualia*, but this is not the accepted view. Understood as intrinsic features of experience or raw feels, *qualia* present problems for **physicalism** and **functionalism** because they seem to be irreducible and non-physical (**knowledge argument**). Recently, proponents of **representationalism about consciousness** suggested a different understanding of what *qualia* are and a possible route for their **reduction.**

Quantum Theories of Consciousness: locate (**phenomenal**) **consciousness** at the level of quantum phenomena (the best known proposal belongs to physicist Roger Penrose and anaesthesiologist Stuart Hameroff). Its motivations include the non-algorithmic character of human thought (which must rely on a non-algorithmic physical process), the difficulty with explaining consciousness within the present theoretical framework and avoidance of **epiphenomenalism.** The suggested physical process is the collapse of the quantum mechanical wave function (the transition of a quantum system from a superposition of wave functions to a single definite state). Quantum self-collapse (collapse not initiated by an act of measurement), the physical correlate of **consciousness,** occurs in the microtubules of **neurons'** cell bodies or dendrites which form coherent structures across the **brain** via gap junctions (bypassing synaptic transmission). Critics doubt the connection between consciousness and quantum mechanics which skips a few levels of description and leads to **panpsychism.**

Further reading: Penrose (1994)

Quine, Willard Van Orman (1908–2000): American philosopher and logician associated with **logical behaviourism**. Always concerned with how scientific theories make 'ontological commitments' to the existence of certain entities, Quine questioned **logical positivism**'s view that a true theory must be a collection of analytic statements where the predicate is contained in the definition of the subject. He argued for verification **holism**: no hypothesis can be tested in isolation from other theoretical statements, including statements about observable phenomena, which are themselves theoretic. Changes introduced by accommodating new data ramify through the whole theory, and the notion of synonymy underlying analyticity cannot be formulated clearly. All theoretical statements are contingent and based on our deeply entrenched beliefs about the world. Quine's **behaviourism** is the view that meaning is exhausted by observable behaviour and should not be explained in terms of internal mental entities. Children associate sentences they hear from adults with different situations and learn to apply terms of a natural language to their internal states (stimulus generalisation constrained by subjective similarity spaces), hence the ideas of **radical interpretation, indeterminacy of translation** and **inscrutability of reference**. The observer-relative nature of psychological language prevents its incorporation into natural science. One must either accept its indispensability and reject **physicalism** or accept physicalism and reject the possibility of **intentional** science (that is **intensional** or sensitive to particular descriptions). Proponents of **eliminative materialism** opted for the second horn of *Quine's dilemma*, but Quine's own views were closer to the **identity theory**, and in his late work he embraced **anomalous monism** ('conceptual **dualism**').

Further reading: Quine (1953, 1960)

Radical Interpretation: the thesis developed by **Quine** and **Davidson** that the ascription of meanings to individual words of a language is derivative from the ascription of meanings to all words of that language. Because the ascription of **mental states** is similarly **holistic**, mental states would be exhaustively ascribed to individuals by a radical interpreter having at his disposal complete behavioural linguistic evidence (**interpretivism**). As interpretation is thought to be radical (from zero) and taking place within a different *linguistic* medium, the **indeterminacy of translation** follows.

Ramsey Sentence: a technical device for non-circular analysis of theoretical terms invented by British mathematician Frank P. Ramsey (1903–30). In a Ramsey sentence a term of a scientific theory is replaced with a variable and all statements containing the replaced term are existentially quantified. Thus, instead of saying that electrons attract protons and so on, one says that there is something that attracts protons (and has certain other properties). In the Ramsey sentence of a whole theory all its specific terms are replaced with their functional definitions or specifications of their causal roles within that theory (*Ramsification*). This allows for their identification with the occupiers of the corresponding causal roles, if any.

Rationalism (nativism, Cartesianism): the view that much of our **knowledge** is **innate**. Rationalism involves psychological and epistemological theses; both were originated in **modern philosophy** by **Descartes** and radicalised by

Malebranche, Spinoza and **Leibniz**. Descartes argued that pure sense experience cannot by itself represent external objects and requires structuring by innate **ideas** distinguished by what they represent (**Brentano** mentions Descartes as a major source for thinking about **intentionality**). But he also held that true knowledge has an a priori character in that it can be built on the foundation of clear and distinct ideas in the manner of mathematical deduction. In the twentieth century, after a period of **behaviourism**'s dominance, the psychological thesis was revived in **Chomsky**'s theory of universal grammar and **Fodor**'s **language of thought** hypothesis. The epistemological thesis, shattered by **Quine**, was reinstated by **Kripke** and other philosophers emphasising the importance of a priori analysis.

Rationality: coherence in one's system of beliefs (theoretical rationality); consistency of one's **actions** with one's beliefs (practical rationality). Rationality as the capacity for drawing justified inferences was always seen as definitive of human **intelligence** (its connection with **logic** was already stated by **Aristotle**). More recently, several philosophers stressed that the attribution of **intentional states** to other people in explaining their behaviour requires seeing them as rational as is possible in the circumstances. Even though people often behave irrationally, they can be intelligible to others only if a certain degree of coherence is presupposed in their belief systems (**holism**). Rationality is thus linked to **normativity**, and for **Davidson** it becomes a Kantian synthetic a priori that cannot be analysed in physical terms and explains the irreducibility of **mental concepts**. However, other philosophers disagree that there can be no codified theory of rationality, especially if one considers that, not being ideally rational, humans remain believers and decision-makers. This realisation led to the development of theories of *bounded rationality* and 'dual-process theories' of reasoning. Although people do not have perfect logical ability, drawing invalid inferences (affirming the consequent: if P then Q, Q, therefore P) and failing deductive (**Wason selection task**) and probabilistic (stereotyping) reasoning tasks, they often manage to believe and behave rationally for the circumstances. But finite agents with limited **memory** and a lack of information, time or cognitive resources to engage in complex calculations cannot always use infallible algorithms and must rely on mental models, biases and **heuristics**. Still, this does not eliminate the need to explain the irrationality of **delusion,** wishful thinking, **self-deception** and weakness of **will.**

Further reading: Mele and Rawling (2004)

Raw Feels see *qualia*

Realism: to be a realist about *X* is to hold that *X* is something real in the sense that its existence does not depend on its being our mental or social construct. As such, it may defy **reduction** and should be admitted into scientific explanation. In **intentional** realism, *X* = intentional **mental states** (beliefs, desires). In **phenomenal** realism, *X* = *qualia*.

Reasons and Causes see **Action**

Recognitional Concepts see **Pragmatism**

Recursive: allowing one to form an infinite range of expressions from a finite set of elements by recurrent application of structure-sensitive rules. The recursive character of human **thought and language** can be seen in our ability to form and process strings like 'The man that chased the dog that chased the cat that chased the mouse tripped and fell' by assigning to them correct subject-predicate relations (it was the man who fell, not the mouse).

Reduction: identification of a higher-order property with a lower-order property (for example, temperature in gases is mean molecular kinetic energy). One may distinguish between ontological reduction (saying that X is Y in the world's **ontology**), conceptual or a priori reduction (saying that **concept** X picks out the same property as concept Y) and **intertheoretic reduction.**

Reductionism (reductivism): to be a reductionist about X is to hold that X is nothing other than some different kind of thing. The term is often reserved for **reductive physicalism,** although **behaviourism, functionalism, functional role semantics** and **naturalised semantics** can all be considered as reductive approaches (about **mental properties** and **content** respectively).

Reductive Physicalism: the view that **mental properties** are physical properties. Its main versions are the **identity theory** and the functional **reduction** of **Armstrong** and **Lewis. Kim** argues that only reductive physicalism can make sense of **mental causation.** He accepts Lewis's restricted identities and shows how the argument from **multiple realisability** and **special sciences** can be turned against itself. The argument says that a mental property (like **pain**) can be realised in physically different systems, and thus cannot be identified with a disjunction of realising its physical properties because disjunctions do not constitute **natural kinds.** But if one accepts that physically different systems are systems where diverse causal principles are in operation, that mental properties have the causal powers of their realisers (**causal inheritance principle**) and that natural kinds are individuated by their causal powers, the implication is that mental properties do not constitute natural kinds either. It follows that there is no psychology as a general science, that scientific psychology is only possible for individual species or organism types. What then is the status of mental properties? Kim concludes that there are no mental properties (no such thing as pain in general) but only **mental concepts**, thus coming close to **eliminativism**. However, this raises questions: if there are no mental properties, what are our mental concepts concepts of? how can we explain the continuity between species and the validity of comparative psychology? The task for a reductionist thus becomes to reduce mental properties without eliminating them. This might be achieved by: (1) accepting **realism** about higher-order properties (Lewis, **Jackson**); (2) holding that there must be a single property underlying the disjunction (once contemplated by Kim); (3) weakening the connection between natural kinds and complete causal homogeneity (Ned Block).

Further reading: Block (1997); Kim (2002)

Reference see **Sense and Reference**

Referential Opacity see **Propositional Attitudes**

Reification: consideration of something for which there is a noun in the language as if at were a real entity (*res* – thing) whereas it may in fact be a process, a nonentity, a mental construct.

Relativism: the view that the way people perceive and think about the world is determined by the language they speak (linguistic relativism) or the practices of their community (cultural or conceptual relativism), and that **knowledge**

and truth are relative to the perspective of one's culture (epistemological relativism).

Representation: that which stands for something else within a different medium. A photograph can be a representation of a building, not being a building itself. Similarly, **mental states** can represent the external world's objects, properties and relations while being entities internal to the **mind**. Representation is central to understanding **intentionality** in a naturalistic way. Instead of thinking that the mind is directed towards some abstract entities like propositions, one can understand **propositional attitudes** (beliefs, desires) as mental phenomena and extend the class of **intentional states**. However, one must be careful to distinguish between the *contents* and the *vehicles* of representations. Whereas the vehicle of a representation is a certain **brain** state, its **content** is that which the representation is about. Understanding representations as internal **information**-carrying states mediating between psychological processes in virtue of their contents is central to **cognitive science**. But there is also the problem of form: *how* do minds/brains represent? The **language of thought** (LOT) hypothesis says that mental representation is symbolic. It is thus *discrete* or *digital* because each symbol has specific content. But in *analogue* or *continuous* representation specific contents cannot be assigned to individual parts (this understanding differs from the original notion introduced to explain **non-conceptual content**). Opponents of LOT argue for the continuous nature of mental representation holding that minds represent the way pictures or holograms do (**image theory, imagery**) and the way maps do (**analytic functionalism**); that representation is *distributed* over subsymbolic units (**connectionism**) or systems larger than an organism (**dynamical systems, extended mind**).

Further reading: Dietrich and Markman (2003)

Representational Theory of Mind (RTM): the view that **intentional states** (thoughts, beliefs, etc.) represent the world (actual or possible) and are semantically evaluable (may be true or false). Anticipated by **Plato, Aristotle,** Ockham and early modern **representationalism,** RTM, which is the main thesis of classical **cognitive science,** is the view that a **language of thought** is the medium of mental **representation.**

Further reading: Sterelny (1990)

Representationalism: the theory of **perception** (particularly **vision**) which holds that perceptual processes are computational-inferential processes that deliver **representations** of distal objects and properties on the basis of proximal (retinal) stimulations. Historically, the view that the **mind** operates on representations – the precursor of the **representational theory of mind** – is found in **Descartes, Malebranche, Locke** and **Hume.** According to it perception is the process whereby the **mind** receives its sensations or particular **ideas** of things. These were thought to be picture-like mental copies of external objects, which rendered perception *indirect*: access to the world was access to one's representations of it. The view was attacked by Arnauld, Foucher, **Berkeley** and Reid, who rejected mental representations and argued that it created the **veil of perception,** leaving the mind out of touch with reality. Today representationalism is the leading approach to perception, though the issue of *immediate* objects of perceptual experience separates its two varieties. *Direct representationalism* holds that we perceive the external world *through* our representations of it. Its proponents escape the veil by accepting **direct realism** (as does, for example, Andrew Brook), and it is often combined with **representationalism about consciousness.** In contrast, *indirect representationalism* emphasises the similarity between veridical and non-veridical perception with respect to internal processes (the argument from **illusion**) and holds that we perceive brain-generated picture-like representations, the end products of causal processes beginning at the retina (direct **brain** stimulation can result in visual experience). It thus bears a certain resemblance to the **sense-datum theory**, and it is not surprising that Descartes and Locke are often mentioned as the precursors of the latter as well.

Representationalism about Consciousness (intentionalism): although the phrase is also used to include **higher-order theories** of **consciousness**, more commonly it designates the view that **phenomenal** states are representational or **intentional states** wholly determined by what they represent, by their **content** (**Dretske**, Michael Tye, Gilbert Harman, **Jackson**). It reconsiders the nature of *qualia*, viewing them not as intrinsic properties of experience but as properties of external objects that experience represents these objects as having: every phenomenal difference implies representational difference. It views sensory experience as *transparent* or *diaphanous*, giving us access to the world via our **representations** of it and allowing us to form beliefs about it. Connecting **phenomenal consciousness** with **intentionality**, representationalism gives the former a clear biological function and is in a position to reconcile it with **physicalism**. However, some philosophers doubt that it can be extended to other phenomenal states like **sensations** or **emotions** (orgasm, anxiety, **pain**) and give counterexamples to its account of perceptual states (**inverted Earth**). In order to account for differences between conscious and non-conscious representation, representation in **perception** and belief and representation in different sensory modalities, one may need to distinguish between *pure representationalism* which identifies any phenomenal property with the property of representing a certain content and more commonly held (implicitly or explicitly) *impure representationalism* which in addition includes 'intentional modes' or 'manners of representation' such as representing a content visually perceptually. David Chalmers argues that because drawing these finer distinctions seems to require the notion of phenomenal representation, representationalism cannot accomplish the **reduction** of the phenomenal. Chalmers and other philosophers also object to representationalism's commitment to **externalism,** holding that the the phenomenal character of experience must be fixed internally.

Further reading: Dretske (1995); Tye (1995); Chalmers (2004)

Rigid Designator see **Causal Theory of Reference**

Russell, Bertrand (1872–1970): English philosopher and logician, one of the founders of analytical philosophy. In 'On denoting' (1905) Russell formulated three puzzles about denotation (hence **intentionality**), observing that *denoting phrases* (indefinite and definite descriptions) do not always denote existing entities. But how can one truly believe of a non-existent individual (like the present King of France) that it does not exist if using a denoting phrase presupposes its existence (the puzzle of true negative existential beliefs)? A related puzzle concerns the violation of the law of identity in contexts created by **propositional attitudes.** To eliminate the view that something is always denoted by such phrases, Russell proposed to analyse statements of the form 'the F is G' as statements whose logical form is: 'there is an x such that Fx, and for any y, if Fy then $y = x$, and Gx'. He also proposed that some names are abbreviated definite descriptions (thus 'Apollo' abbreviates 'the sun-god') and in *Principia Mathematica* extended this analysis (*theory of definite descriptions*) to all proper names. This was motivated by his distinction between *knowledge by acquaintance* and *knowledge by description*, and the view that genuine **singular** thoughts involve direct acquaintance with individuals, hence that the only *logically proper names* (names referring directly to objects) are words for the immediately experienced **sense-data** ('this', 'that') and **universals**. These considerations later led him to **phenomenalism**, and then **neutral monism**.

Further reading: Russell (1956)

Ryle, Gilbert (1900–76): English philosopher, the founder of **logical behaviourism**. Ryle launched an attack against **Cartesian** substance **dualism** which views the **mind** as a special 'kind of existence' to which we have **privileged access**. But this view was undermined by **Freud**, and Ryle calls it 'the dogma of the ghost in the machine'. It commits a **category mistake** by claiming that internal processes stand behind a person's behaviour. In contrast Ryle argues that having a mind is having behavioural **dispositions** or **knowledge-how**, and illustrates this with the example of **intelligence**: are there any criteria of intelligence other than intelligent behaviour?

Further reading: Ryle (1949)

Ryle's Regress (homunculus argument): a problem for **representationalism**, and by extension the **computational** and **representational theory of mind**, inspired by **Ryle's** arguments. If the **mind** operates on **representations**, then there must be someone who interprets them, and so one has to postulate a homunculus (a tiny person) inside the head for the result of every causal representation-transformational process, thus resulting in an infinite regress. The problem has several aspects: (1) the difficulty one has with understanding how physical entities can carry and read off **information** (but consider DNA); (2) the fear that it will lead one to postulate the Cartesian **self**; and (3) the suspicion that positing internal representations does not really explain perceptual experience like seeing.

S

Sartre, Jean-Paul (1905–80): French philosopher who developed an existentialist version of **phenomenology**. Concerned with the issues of **intentionality** and **consciousness**, Sartre began with studying **imagination** where the relation of consciousness to the non-existent is the most evident. He opposed **Husserl**, whom he interpreted as holding that reality is immanent to consciousness, and later introduced the categories of the in-itself (*en-soi*), the transphenomenal being of things extending beyond appearances, and the for-itself (*pour-soi*) or consciousness constantly reconstituting the **phenomenal** being including itself. With the *pour-soi* nothingness comes into being because it is the nihilation (*néantisation*) of the *en-soi*: looking for someone who is not there we introduce nothingness into the otherwise complete being. Sartre's understanding of consciousness as non-substantial (one is not a **self** but a presence-to-self) underlies his views on absolute human freedom: at every moment one has to 'choose oneself' and is the true author of one's **actions**. Thinking that one's actions are determined by one's external situation or one's internal nature is a kind of **self-deception**, bad faith (*mauvaise foi*) which leads to anguish.

Further reading: Sartre [1943] (1953)

Scepticism: to be a sceptic about *X* is to deny that it exists because **knowledge** of its existence is impossible. Scepticism was a school of thought in **ancient philosophy**

(founded by Pyrrho of Elis, *c.*361–270 BC, developed by Aenesidemus of Cnossos and Sextus Empiricus) which criticised any attempt (particularly that of the Stoics) to go beyond appearances. Another school, Academic scepticism (founded by Arcesilaus in the 200s BC) was less radical in its outlook and concentrated on uncovering difficulties in various philosophical positions.

Schizophrenia: mental disorder characterised by abnormal thought, **perception, mood,** emotional experience and behaviour. **Delusions** are characteristic of paranoid schizophrenia. Thus people suffering from *Capgras delusion* fail to recognise their acquaintances, believing that they have been replaced by impostors, and those suffering from the *thought insertion delusion* believe that their thoughts are not their own. Its other symptoms include auditory **hallucinations** (hearing voices), social withdrawal (impaired **theory of mind**) and difficulty with forming a stable **self**-conception. It is unclear whether different forms of schizophrenia constitute a single disorder, but there seems to be a progressive worsening in the **unity of consciousness** to the stage where patients appear unaware of temporal and spacial unity between objects or are even unable to represent unified objects. Reproducing the original insight of Eugen Bleuler who described schizophrenia as a 'splitting of the psychic functions' (1911), some researchers suggest today that schizophrenia results from the disrupted integrity of neural circuits.

Searle, John R. (b.1932): American philosopher of language and **mind,** for whom the central notion is that of **consciousness.** Searle rejects the **mind–body problem** formulated in terms of whether mental phenomena are physical or non-physical, and advocates *biological naturalism,* according to which conscious mental phenomena are higher-level features of the **brain,** both caused by neu-robiological processes and irreducibly subjective (close to **emergentism**). This view underlies his understanding of **intentionality.** By Searle's 'connection principle' **intentional states** can be **unconscious** only if they are in principle available to subjective awareness. Thus only (potentially) conscious states possess intrinsic, as opposed to interpreter-relative, intentionality. Intentional states are distinguished by their *aspectual shape* (**intensionality**), they represent things under an aspect (desire for water is different from desire for H_2O), but the determination of aspectual shape is only possible for conscious states. Because Searle recognises only two types of processes in the mind/brain – intentional or subjective and brutally neurophysiological – he is also a major critic of **functionalism** (the **Background**), the **computational theory of mind** (**Chinese room**), and later, the very notion of **computation.**

Further reading: Searle (1992)

Secondary Qualities see **Primary and Secondary Qualities**

Self, The: that to which each of us presumably refers when saying 'I', which ensures our **unity of consciousness** and **personal identity,** which possibly survives the destruction of the body, the soul. Conceiving of the **mind** as surviving the annihilation of the physical world, **Descartes** made the **self,** a simple indivisible thinking substance (*Cartesian ego*), a major topic in **modern philosophy.** Similar views existed long before Descartes in many religious traditions, and his *cogito* argument was anticipated by Avicenna's 'flying man' suddenly coming into existence with full awareness of his self but no **sensation** coming from the external world as he is suspended in an empty space. But as Descartes also originated **representationalism,** the conception of the conscious self as the bearer of sensations and **ideas** (labelled by **Dennett** 'the Cartesian theatre view of **consciousness**') proved extremely persistent. Holding that the self cannot be given in **perception** and we can form no idea of it, **Berkeley**, however, admitted it into his philosophy as the notion we have of our awareness of ideas, necessary for understanding the human **person** but not given to us with clarity. And, although **Hume** denied the existence of a single unified self, noting that he can never catch himself without a perception and concluding that there is nothing to the mind beyond a bundle of individual states (*bundle theory of the self*), the idea of the self being a product of **imagination**, he remained dissatisfied with his solution. **Kant**, who shared Hume's **scepticism** about the empirical ego, acknowledged that the pure ego ('I think') must accompany all conscious experience as a **transcendental** principle. Today, when substance **dualism** no longer seems acceptable in the scientific picture of the world, the problem becomes to understand **self-consciousness** without postulating the enduring self.

Self-Consciousness: awareness of oneself. In **modern philosophy** through **Brentano** to **phenomenology** this often implied being aware of one's **self** as the subject of experiences and the author of thoughts and **actions**. While this classical view sees reflexive awareness of one's **mental states** or *apperception* (**Leibniz**'s term) as inseparable from and necessary for genuine **consciousness**, analytical philosophy mostly concentrated on the semantic problem of *de se* beliefs and the question of **self-knowledge**. Recently **higher-order theories** returned to the issue of what makes mental states conscious, while other researchers addressed the nature of our self-**concept**. These two problems were also shaped by **Descartes**: (1) we can think of our bodies, but not our **minds**, as aggregates of parts, for taking anything away from our minds seems inconceivable; and (2) 'inner awareness of one's thought and existence is so innate . . . that . . . we cannot fail to have it'. To escape substance **dualism**, the best strategy might be to argue for **eliminativism** about the self (**Dennett**): nothing real corresponds to our self-concept which emerges from the chaining together of various **contents** by **cognitive** subsystems as an ongoing narrative. But one should be careful not to eliminate with it our sense of the self whose disruption may underlie **autism, schizophrenia** and **multiple personality** disorders. Besides, a bundle of contents cannot itself create self-perspectivalness which is a basic psychological property of experiencing organisms, and understanding self-consciousness through the mastery of the first-person pronoun is misleading (Susan Hurley, José Luis Bermúdez). Organisms' capacity to navigate and explore their environments already requires that they represent objects and locations relative to themselves, the experiencing subjects (the ecological self).

Further reading: Bermúdez (1998); Metzinger (2003)

Self-Deception: failure to acknowledge to oneself a truth because of the interference of one's other interests (for example, refusing to admit that one is being deceived by a dear person despite all the evidence pointing to it). The paradox of self-deception results when one considers that ordinary deception requires two agents, only one of whom knows the truth: how can the same agent both know and not know a truth? One solution is to partition the **self** following **Freud**. Another is to hold that such people do not have contradictory beliefs but fail to arrive at the correct conclusion.

Further reading: Mele (2001)

Self-Knowledge: knowledge of one's own **mental states**. Following **Descartes** is was often held that our **knowledge** of our conscious **mind** is epistemically privileged in comparison with other kinds of knowledge (**privileged access**). It appears direct, unmediated, non-inferential and thus certain, secure and even infallible. We obtain it via **introspection** and are the ultimate judges of the **content** of our conscious states (**first-person authority**). For Descartes, such was our knowledge of the persisting **self**. This view was criticised by **Kant** who argued that we can know only how we represent ourselves to be, not how we really are. It was further attacked by **Freud, James, Ryle, Wittgenstein** and **Sellars**. But they showed that our minds are not completely transparent to us, which leaves it open whether some conscious states may have a special status. We can be mistaken about our internal states: people often have false beliefs about their desires and motivations, they misidentify their **emotions** and rationalise their reasoning and choice. But there is a different twist to the idea that being in a mental state we know that we are in it. Sydney Shoemaker noted that one cannot fail to refer to oneself or be mistaken about oneself (*I*) being in some mental state ('*I* am having such and such experience). This 'immunity to error through misidentification relative to the first-person pronoun' suggests important connections between **self-consciousness** and **rationality**. Self-knowledge is also addressed in the **externalism–internalism** debate with internalists arguing that externalism is incompatible with self-knowledge because our knowledge of our thoughts seems unaffected by the environment we are in.

Further reading: Shoemaker (1994); Ludlow and Martin (1998)

Sellars, Wilfrid (1912–89): American philosopher, the first proponent of **functional role semantics** (about language). His interest was in the discrepancy between 'the scientific image of man' and the *manifest image* that we have of ourselves as perceivers of a three-dimensional coloured world, thinkers and agents, and that is found in the *perennial philosophy* which takes elements of the manifest image for real features of the world. This underlined his earlier rejection of the **myth of the given**, and his view that awareness (sapience or reflexive **consciousness** as distinct from mere sentience or **sensation**) and thought are 'linguistic affairs'.

Further reading: Sellars (1963)

Semantics: (1) the study of relations between mental **representations** and their meaning or **content** (*psychosemantics*); (2) possession of content by mental representations.

Sensations: (1) bodily states (called 'feelings' in discussions of **emotions**) like **pains**, itches, tickles, pangs, throbs, tingles, burnings, hunger, thirst, nausea, experience of warmth and cold, etc. caused by physiological changes. One much debated issue is whether in addition to their **phenomenal** feels (*qualia*) sensations also have representational **content** (consider proprioception, the sensation of body position and movement); (2) as used in earlier discussions of **perception**, that which is delivered by sense experience.

Sense and Reference: two components of meaning isolated by **Frege**. Reference is the relation between an expression and that object or property that it picks out in the world, whereas sense is the manner in which it does so. For Frege, sense determines reference, because senses are had by propositions rather than their constituents. The causal theory of reference challenges Frege's view. This distinction is paralleled by those between **intension** and **extension**, connotation and denotation, and **cognitive** and **intentional** mental **content**.

Sense-Data: sensible qualities, quite literally data, presented by the senses to **consciousness**. In later versions of the **sense-datum theory** they are taken to be **mental objects** or private entities given to the **mind**.

Sense-Datum Theory: the theory of **perception** (primarily **vision**) which holds that the immediate objects of one's awareness in perceptual experience are **sense-data** rather than ordinary physical objects. Appearing in early **modern philosophy**, it became prominent in the early twentieth century in the work of G. E. Moore and C. D. Broad and was dominant until recently, counting among its advocates Frank **Jackson** and presently Howard Robinson. The theory builds on the following premises: (1) that of which a person is aware in perceptual experience is the object of experience; and (2) veridical and non-veridical perceptual experiences feel subjectively the same (the argument from **illusion**). Because we cannot be sure that objects and properties that experience presents us with really exist (secondary qualities), it concludes that there must be certain private non-physical entities which constitute the immediate object of one's perceptual experiences, have the experienced qualities (*qualia*) and are revealed in **introspection**. It opposes direct **representationalism** in emphasising the **phenomenal** nature of experience. However, the theory, whose critics include **Austin** and **Place**, is problematic because the nature of sense-data and their relation to physical objects and perceivers' neural states is obscure, it leads to (attribute) **dualism**, it creates the **veil of perception**, it commits the **phenomenological fallacy**

and it disrupts the connection between perception and **knowledge** of the external world.

Further reading: Jackson (1977)

Sententialism see **Language of Thought**

Silicon Chip Replacement: a **thought experiment** devised by Zenon Pylyshyn to argue against **Searle's** view that the **brain's** biological properties are essential for mentality. For any **mental state** (like **pain**) one can imagine that the participating **neurons** are replaced one by one with silicon chip prostheses so that the causal properties of the total integrated circuit are preserved. After all the neurons have been replaced, the mental state will not change its identity, which suggests that it is causal, not biological, properties that underlie the workings of the **mind**.

Further reading: Pylyshyn (1984)

Simulation Theory: the view, opposed to the **theory theory,** that our understanding of **other minds** is not mediated by a **theory of mind,** but involves imaginative simulation of others' mental processes that we would have in similar situations (Jane Heal, Robert Gordon, Alvin Goldman). However, it has to explain how we manage to master **mental concepts** and know our own **mental states.** Some researchers hold that it complements the theory theory rather than opposes it, and others find support for it in the discovery of **mirror neurons** (but more recent evidence suggests that empathy and theory of mind are subserved by different, although overlapping, **brain** systems).

Further reading: Carruthers and Smith (1996)

Singular: about a concrete particular.

Situated Cognition see **Embedded Cognition**

Smart, John J. C. (b.1920): English-born Australian philosopher, one of the originators of the **identity theory**. Initially a proponent of **logical behaviourism,** he was converted by **Place,** made prominent the notion of identity in the formulation of the theory and generalised it to **propositional attitudes** (beliefs, desires). He proposed to analyse **sensation** reports in *topic-neutral* terms ('there is something going on which is like what is going on when . . . ') to explain how introspectable sensations can be identical with **brain** processes, thus paving the way for the **causal theory of mind.**

Further reading: Smart (1959)

Solipsism: the belief that only one's own **mind** and immediate experience really exist.

Soul see **Person**

Spandrel see **Evolution**

Special Sciences: elaboration of the **multiple realisability** argument by **Fodor. Reductionism** is too strong a constraint on the **unity of science** if it requires that acceptable theories in the special sciences (geology, economics, psychology) be ultimately reducible to physics (as implies **Nagelian reduction**). Special sciences employ predicates which are unique to them and allow them to formulate counterfactual-supporting generalisations about events whose physical realisations may have nothing in common (one can make generalisations about monetary exchanges irrespective of the physical nature of the stuff that functions as money in different communities). Special sciences are *autonomous* and irreducible because higher-order properties they deal with are multiply realisable at lower physical levels, such that none of them (like the property of being a mountain) may be identified with a single physical property. But identifying a higher-order property with a (potentially open-ended) disjunction of physical properties realising it is also an unacceptable solution because disjunctions cannot form **natural kinds**. Thus, if psychological properties are multiply realisable (across species and, due to neural **plasticity**, within the same species or the same individual), *psychology* is autonomous from and irreducible to neurology.

Further reading: Fodor (1974)

Spinoza, Baruch (Benedict) (1632–77): Dutch Jewish philosopher, the originator of attribute **dualism**. Spinoza questioned **Descartes'** premise that a substance must have only one defining attribute, and argued that there can be only one substance or self-subsistent being, which is God, for everything owes its existence to Him. But God is not distinct from nature, and every individual existent is a mode or state (*affectio*) of this only substance, God or nature (*deus sive natura*). It presents itself to reason under the attributes of thought and extension, as **mind** and matter, which are different aspects or parallel expressions of the same reality (**parallelism**). This truth can be grasped by reason when, analysing the order and relation of **ideas** identical to those of things, it arrives at the complete idea of God (**rationalism**). Desires and **emotions** (bodily affects or modifications, *corporis affectiones*) prevent one from realising the true causes of things and the necessary character of all events. But by understanding their motivations, people can begin to control and modify their emotions (Spinoza's psychological psychiatry).

Further reading: Spinoza (1994)

Split Brains: the existence of two dissociable centres of **consciousness** in patients after 'brain bisection' operations or commisurotomy (surgical severance of the corpus callosum, the great commissure consisting of axons connecting the cortex of the two hemispheres, practised in the 1960s to prevent epileptic activity spreading from one hemisphere to the other). The dissociation appears in carefully controlled conditions when visual stimuli are presented to only one hemisphere. Because the left hemisphere controls speech in most people, such patients become unable to describe anything to the left of their visual fixation points (they say they see nothing or deny that there is anything in their left hand) without appearing disturbed by it. These studies, showing 'two independent brains' controlling different halves of the body, questioned the existence of the unifying **self** and provoked much discussion about **personal identity**: are there two **persons** in one body? one person split between two bodies? or is there a one and a half persons? Outside the laboratory, however, split-brains people usually show no disturbance of the **unity of consciousness**, retaining awareness of themselves as subjects.

Further reading: Nagel (1971)

Strawson, Peter F. (1919–2006): English philosopher who defended the ordinary view of the world against **scepticism** and the *revisionary metaphysics* of philosophers like **Sellars**. (This term of Strawson's is now commonly applied to **eliminative materialism**.) Philosophical reflection should begin with taking for granted the background framework of our thought: distinguishing **persons** from bodies and viewing the concept of person as primitive, admitting that in **perception** we are immediately aware of **mind**-external things, or noticing that being self-conscious requires recognising the **self-consciousness** of others.

Further reading: Strawson (1959)

Strong AI see **Artificial Intelligence**

Subdoxastic: that of which a person cannot be aware in belief (*doxa*). Subdoxastic states are subpersonal states characterising low-level **information** processing.

Subliminal: below the threshold of conscious **perception.**

Substance Dualism see **Dualism**

Supervenience: a relation of dependence between two (sets of) properties: B supervenes on A iff whenever A is instantiated, B is instantiated too. The notion is employed in **externalism–internalism** debates and discussions of the **mind–body problem** where it was introduced by **Davidson (anomalous monism)** to capture the idea of dependence without reducibility. To say that the mental supervenes on the physical is to say that the physical nature of a thing or event wholly determines its **mental properties,** that there is no mental difference without physical difference. This can be elaborated in several ways. Thus *weak supervenience* is the claim that, for every **possible world,** if two entities are physically indistinguishable, they are also mentally indistinguishable. But this notion is too weak for **physicalism,** because, applying to only one world, it permits worlds, physically like ours, where amoebae have mentality but humans haven't. Thus one needs *strong supervenience* – the claim that for any individuals x and y and worlds w_1 and w_2 if these individuals in their respective worlds are physically indistinguishable, they are also mentally indistinguishable. This idea and the notion of **supervenience base** were used by proponents of **non-reductive physicalism** to argue for the reality of **mental causation** as *supervenient causation.* But because of the problem of mental causation, one may argue for *global supervenience* – the claim that any two worlds that are physically indistinguishable are mentally indistinguishable (though **Kim** holds that it does not avoid the problem). Finally, *supervenience physicalism* is the thesis that physicalism is true if, and only if, every world that is a minimal (nothing added) physical duplicate of the actual world is its duplicate *simpliciter* (**Jackson**).

Further reading: Kim (1993); Jackson (1993)

Supervenience Argument see **Mental Causation**

Supervenience base (subvenient physical base:) a (open-ended) series of physical properties the instantiation of each of which is sufficient for the instantiation of a given **mental property.**

Supervenient Behaviourism see **Logical Behaviourism**

Swampman: a creature invented by **Davidson** to test his theory of meaning, but often used to argue against **externalism, teleological functionalism** and the **teleological theory of content.** Swampman comes into existence after lightning hits a tree and is an exact physical replica of Davidson so nobody can tell one from the other. Historical theories must deny him **intentional states** because he does not have any evolutionary or developmental history, and many people find this conclusion counterintuitive.

Further reading: Davidson (1987)

Symbol Grounding Problem: the problem for the **computational theory of mind** formulated by Steven Harnad. Even if the **mind** is a symbol-manipulating device, one must explain how meaning or **content** attaches to symbols. For

Harnad, the meaning of symbols must be grounded in sensorimotor capacities (robotic functions) and the **phenomenal** character of experience, which may be the **brain**'s solution to the problem, but the CTM has no resources to capture that.

Further reading: Harnad (1990)

Synaesthesia: a condition in which the **perception** of a certain kind of stimuli is systematically accompanied by normally unrelated perceptual experiences from the same or a different sensory modality (letters or musical notes are perceived as having their own **colours**). Its existence supports the privileged status of phenomenal **self-knowledge** and may pose problems for **representationalism about consciousness**.

Syntactic Engine: according to some philosophers, the **mind** understood from the perspective of scientific psychology. Stephen Stich argued that if the **computational theory of mind** is right and if **intentional states** (beliefs, desires) have **broad content**, then **content** is irrelevant to psychological explanation. Scientific psychology must provide a causal explanation of what happens inside the mind/**brain** but broad contents fail to supervene on physiology. Thus **folk psychology**'s appeal to the content of **mental states** in explaining behaviour (John stretched his hand towards the bottle because he wanted to drink and thought that there was water in the bottle) is unscientific, and **cognitive psychology** should not individuate mental states by their semantic properties. Besides, such **individuation** is impossible because of the **holism** and pragmatic sensitivity of content attribution (when we say that someone wants or believes something we invoke a similarity judgement which is vague and context-dependent). Thus even narrow content cannot help the **representational theory of mind,** and viewing the mind as a *semantic engine* is mistaken. Stich called this the *principle of psychological autonomy*; it is also known as the *syntactic theory of the mind,* and is nothing other than **eliminativism** about content. The approach was adopted by proponents of **eliminative materialism** and later modified through their acceptance of **connectionism** (but Stich always accepted the autonomy of psychology and later criticised eliminativism about **mental concepts**).

Further reading: Stich (1983)

Systematicity: the property of **thought and language** in virtue of which if one can think that Mary loves John one can also think that John loves Mary. The systematicity of thought may require that **representation** in the **mind/ brain** have the form of a **language of thought.**

Further reading: Fodor and Pylyshyn (1988)

Tacit Knowledge: a set of internally represented **innate** knowledge structures that explain our folk non-scientific competence in various domains of experience. Inspired by **Chomsky**'s idea of universal grammar, developmental psychologists proposed theories of folk physics (from infancy people's interaction with objects is guided by the principles of continuity and solidity – Elizabeth Spelke), folk biology (**essentialism** – Frank Keil) and **folk psychology (theory of mind).**

Further reading: Keil (1989); Spelke (1990)

Teleological: involving a purpose, end or goal.

Teleological Functionalism (teleofunctionalism): the variety of **functionalism** which avoids the too liberal assignment of **mental states** by holding that the functional organisation of beings with genuine mentality must be characterised teleologically in terms of functions their states acquired in the course of **evolution**.

Teleological Theory of Content (teleosemantics): uses the notion of biological function to explain how mental **representations** can have **content**. Parts of biological organisms are ascribed functions because their performance contributed to the fitness and survival of these organisms' ancestors. These functions were selected for in the course of **evolution**. That's why the function of the heart is to pump blood and not to make thumping noises. The biological notion of function is teleological and normative: it refers to what parts of organisms are supposed to do and permits the possibility of malfunctioning. Thus mechanisms producing mental representations similarly have the production of certain true representations as their *teleofunctions*. To use the classical example: before the frog snaps its tongue at a fly, its visual system goes into the representational state that corresponds to the presence of a fly (that is its teleofunction). In this way, contents of representational states derive from functions of the mechanisms that produce them. This may seem to solve the problem of **misrepresentation**, but it was argued by **Drctskc** and **Fodor** that because it is indeterminate how one should describe the functions of biological mechanisms, no determinate contents can be assigned to representations produced by them. (What is it exactly that the frog's visual system represents: flies? flies-or-bee-bees? small black moving things?) This is the problem of functional **indeterminacy** similar to the **disjunction problem**. Solutions to it were proposed by Fred Dretske, Ruth

Millikan, David Papineau and Karen Neander. Other problems include **Swampman** and the need to account for **concepts** that have no immediate impact on organisms' fitness.

Theory of Mind (TOM): an implicit theory we employ in explaining other people's behaviour by attributing to them internal states like beliefs and desires **(folk psychology)**. Its existence is defended by the **theory theory** and denied by the **simulation theory**. Within the theory theory researchers are divided between viewing it as a result of our domain-general theory-forming capacity (Josef Perner, Henry Wellman, Alison Gopnik) and viewing it as constituting **tacit knowledge** or even falling under computational **modularity** (Simon Baron-Cohen, Alan Leslie, Gabriel Segal). Discussion centres on 'false-belief tasks' which show that children acquire an understanding of false beliefs only at the age of four or five (three-year-olds do not understand that someone can have a false belief, for example, about where something is). According to Perner, the designer of the task, between the ages of three and four children develop new **concepts** and undergo a major *conceptual change* similar to conceptual change in science. However, this view is problematic as the same pattern is exhibited by all normally developing children regardless of differences in general **intelligence** and **learning** ability. The existence of such correlation is also contradicted by data on **Williams syndrome**.
    Further reading: Carruthers and Smith (1996)

Theory Theory: (1) the view that our understanding of **other minds** is mediated by an implicit theory, the **theory of mind**, which, as **Lewis** noted, resembles a scientific theory in using a number of interconnected theory-specific terms;

(2) a psychological theory of **concepts** according to which concepts are sets of beliefs or mini-theories of categories that they represent in thought (Susan Carey, Frank Keil). However, as a version of semantic **holism**, the theory fails to meet the publicity constraint.

Thought and Language: the view that thought is linguistic, that natural language is necessary for (propositional) thought, as its consequence or condition, is quite widespread. However, this **cognitive** conception of language is relatively new, becoming prominent in the twentieth century and replacing the **image theory**. This view originates with **Frege**'s analysis of the **intentionality** of thought through the logical structure of language and his linguistic **holism** (words have meaning only in the context of a sentence). Thus Michael Dummett holds that language must be primary to thought in the order of explanation because the ascription of thoughts is a matter of interpretation, that only verbalised thought is sufficiently uniform for that purpose, and that verbal formulations cannot adequately represent the **content** of mental processes of languageless creatures who do not possess the requisite **concepts**. But if one ties concept possession to natural language and accepts a public theory of linguistic meaning, one receives a stronger conception which denies languageless thought and even views thought itself as subvocal saying (**behaviourism, Sellars, Davidson, Dennett**). Contrasted with this conception is the communicative conception of language according to which linguistic expressions inherit their semantic properties from thoughts they conventionally express and language must be analysed in terms of speakers' communicative **intentions**. This view, which finds significant empirical support, is particularly associated with **Grice**, but also with

Russell, Lewis, Searle, Fodor and other proponents of the representational theory of mind.

Further reading: Carruthers and Boucher (1998)

Thought Experiment: an experiment done mentally, only with the help of imagination. While thought experiments predicting a certain course of events were also employed in hard sciences, particularly physics, some people feel that many thought experiments in philosophy of mind are unreliable 'intuition pumps'. Although they often help clarify conceptual issues, some of them are too unspecific in detail, for example, to be run as a computer simulation.

Transcendent: beyond the limits of possible experience, unavailable in experience.

Transcendental: (1) constituting a necessary precondition of any experience; (2) concerning transcendent matters.

Transcendental Naturalism: the view that certain philosophical problems cannot be solved because of the natural limitations on human cognitive abilities.

Turing, Alan M. (1912–54): English mathematician, one of the originators of artificial intelligence and the computational theory of mind. Working on computable numbers he described the universal computing machine known as the Turing machine (Alonzo Church's term), the forebearer of the modern digital computer, and later formulated the Turing test to evaluate machine intelligence.

Turing Machine: a device imagined by Turing in developing the notion of computation. A Turing machine consists of an infinitely long tape divided into squares with symbols from a finite alphabet printed in some of them and a reading-writing device which moves along the tape scanning the symbols. The device executes a set of instructions specified in its **machine table** so that upon encountering a certain symbol it can replace it with a different symbol and then move left or right by one square. This way, despite its seeming simplicity, the machine is able to transform any input into any output if the two are related through a computable function.

Turing Test: a behavioural test ('imitation game') devised by **Turing** to determine whether an artificial system possesses **intelligence**. Considering the ability to maintain conversation as a mark of intelligence, Turing proposes that if after interrogating by teletype a human and a machine for a period of time, a human judge cannot tell which is which, the machine should be considered intelligent.

Further reading: Turing (1950)

Twin-Earth: a planet invented by **Putnam** to argue that sense does not determine reference. The argument was initially formulated for linguistic meaning ('meanings just ain't in the *head*'), but Putnam later accepted its extension to psychological states (**externalism**). Twin-Earth is like our Earth in all respects except one: the stuff indistinguishable from water in all its observational properties is not H_2O but a totally different chemical substance XYZ (twin-water). Imagine that Oscar from Earth has an exact internal duplicate on Twin-Earth, Twin-Oscar. Knowing nothing about water's and twin-water's microstructure (the **thought experiment** is set in 1750), they both may think about the substances on their planets under the same description 'colourless, odourless substance found in rivers, lakes and seas, falling from the sky as rain and used by people for drinking'. But Oscar's and Twin-Oscar's seemingly identical beliefs which they both express using the word 'water' ('Water quenches thirst') cannot have the same content because the reference of their 'water' words and their respective psychological states were formed in different physical environments. Because **intentional states** (thoughts, beliefs, desires) are individuated by their truth conditions (and **concepts** – by their **extensions**), it follows that thoughts involving **natural kind** concepts must have environmentally determined **broad content**. In terms of **supervenience**: content does not supervene on neurophysiology because two intrinsically identical individuals may have thoughts with different content. (Although this particular example is unfortunate as human bodies are 60 per cent water, other examples like topaz-citrine avoid this problem.)

Further reading: Putnam (1975); Pessin et al. (1996)

Two-Factor Theories: theories which hold that there are two determinants of **content** of mental **representations** (Hartry Field, Ned Block, Brian Loar, Colin McGinn, William Lycan): the external determinant (specifiable by their causal connections with the environment) and the internal component (their conceptual roles or **narrow content**). The external factor accounts for the possibility of translation and communication, but the internal factor serves the purpose of psychological explanation. The problem, however, is how to make the two factors compatible.

Further reading: Block (1986)

Type/Token Distinction: the distinction between a kind and its individual instances (tokens). Thus the word 'advantage' contains three tokens of the same letter type 'a'.

Unconscious: a state or process is unconscious if it belongs to a low level of **information** processing and is in principle unavailable to subjective awareness or if it is not experienced but could have been had attention been focused on it. A person is considered unconscious if there is no information processing at all and they are non-responsive to themselves or the environment. Without further qualification the term seldom has today the meaning given to it by **Freud**.

Unity of Consciousness: integrated **representation** of the world and oneself which involves simultaneous **phenomenal** awareness of discrete objects with their properties, often detectable through different sensory modalities (seeing a ginger cat and hearing him mewing), their related existence in space and time, one's bodily **sensations**, overall emotional or **mood** state and a flow of conscious thoughts. All these experiences appear unified into a single state of **consciousness** existing against the background of one's self-awareness as their subject. This seems to require the existence of the **self** unifying all the different **contents** of experience, but the tenability of this view was questioned after the discovery of **split brains** and **multiple personalities** phenomena.
　　Further reading: Cleeremans (2003)

Unity of Science: the view associated with **logical positivism** that all sciences can be unified into a single science via the **reduction** of sciences of different levels of reality to the next lower level (psychology–biology–chemistry–physics) so that the laws of microphysics would become the basic laws of all sciences. It was questioned by the **special sciences** argument, but the issue of the extent to which lower-level laws determine higher-level laws remains open.

Universals: properties expressed by general **concepts** and instantiated by different particular things, particulars (every cat instantiates *catness* or the property of *being a cat*). Asking whether genera and species exist in themselves or only in thought, Porphyry (*c*.232–305) formulated the problem of universals for **medieval philosophy**. But its still contemporary significance transpires only in the contrast between **Aquinas' realism** and Ockham's *nominalism*. Like **Aristotle**, Aquinas held that **knowledge** begins with **perception**. Because perception delivers universals, philosophical analysis must go back to particulars separating properties of things known through general concepts. By abstraction the immaterial intellect arrives at the knowledge of the forms. In contrast, William of Ockham (*c*.1285–1349) held that universals exist only in thought. However, his view arguably does not stem from *Ockham's razor*, the principle that 'plurality is not to be posited without necessity'. For Ockham, intuitive **cognition** begins with the direct apprehension of particulars. Noticing similarity between them, abstractive cognition forms general concepts which represent real objects in our mental language (**language of thought**). But no particular is necessary because God could have created things in any other non-contradictory way (**possible worlds**). Leaving aside the theology, one can see how **intentionality** (and the contingency of our perception of similarity) poses difficulties for **non-reductive physicalism** and may motivate a priori **physicalism**.

Further reading: Ockham (1990); Armstrong (1989)

Veil of Perception (~ experience, ~ appearance): the problem for theories of indirect **perception** from which it follows that there is something like a thin film of mental entities separating perceivers from access to the external world.

Veridical see **Perception**

Verificationism: the view, associated with **logical positivism**, that the meaning of a statement expressing a proposition is its conditions of verification.

Vision: sense modality which produces the experience of seeing. Because we receive most **information** about the world through vision (**colour** vision in particular), it is central to debates in philosophy of **perception**, where one must always keep in mind the ambiguity in the verb 'see': registering visual information versus having conscious perception of it; being directed at mind-independent objects versus having visual experience; having versus not having conceptual knowledge of what one sees (**Dretske**'s distinction between epistemic and non-epistemic seeing). Landmarks of vision research include the discovery of orientation-sensitive **neurons**, **Marr**'s computational theory, and the discovery of two visual processing systems, the dorsal and ventral streams (M. Ungerleider and L. Mishkin, M. A. Goodale and A. D. Milner). The dorsal stream (the striate-posterior parietal pathway) codes visuomotor information about objects' spatial properties (shape, size, orientation, location), whereas the ventral stream (the occipital-temporal pathway) processes recognitional

information about objects which allows for their identification. Perceptual control of **action** can be achieved
by the dorsal stream in the absence of conscious awareness, which suggests that visual **phenomenal consciousness** requires the activation of the ventral stream (and
probably intact parietal and frontal pathways subserving attention). Another phenomenon which may throw
light on mechanisms of visual consciousness is *binocular
rivalry*, when different stimuli presented to the two eyes
are experienced as alternating percepts.

Further reading: Noë and Thompson (2002); Goodale
and Milner (2005)

Volition: activity of the **will** manifested in individual acts,
volitions.

von Neumann, John (1903–57): American mathematician,
the designer of the first computers (NORC, MANIAC),
the forebearers of the modern digital computer (stored
program consecutive execution computing device) known
as the *von Neumann machine*.

Wason Selection Task: a psychological tool for testing conditional reasoning (evaluating conditional rules of the form
'if P then Q') designed by Peter Wason in the 1960s. The
subject is presented with four cards, for example 'D', 'F',
'3' and '7', and is asked to determine whether the rule 'if
D is on one side, then 3 is on the other side' holds. The
subject is allowed to turn over only *two* cards. The right
cards are 'D' and '7', but about 90 per cent of subjects

fail the task (usually selecting 'D' and '3'). Curiously, people's performance improves radically if problems with parallel structure have concrete **content** like 'If a person is drinking beer in a bar, then the person should be over 18'. The cards are, correspondingly, 'Is drinking beer', 'Is drinking lemonade', 'Is over 18' and 'Is under 18', and most people give the right answer. One explanation for this content effect is that people's practical reasoning skills are sounder than their theoretical skills. But proponents of **evolutionary psychology** argue that the effect is due to our **cognitive architecture**, namely the evolved domain-specific algorithms pertaining to reasoning about social contracts and reducing risk in hazardous situations. Humans are social animals and must maintain group stability by making sure that it contains no 'free riders', that someone who received a benefit paid a cost. The pressure to keep track of social contracts led to the **evolution** of the *cheater-detection module* whose operation is manifested in the content effects. This conclusion is question by proponents of the relevance theory who hold that the effect is due to the operation of more general pragmatic comprehension mechanisms.

What-It's-Like: Thomas Nagel's characterisation of **consciousness** as that inherently subjective aspect of **mind** which cannot be captured by reductive theories (**physicalism**). A creature is conscious if there is something that it is like to be that creature which cannot be understood from the objective standpoint. In his **knowledge argument, Jackson** modified this criterion applying it to **mental states** rather than whole organisms.

Further reading: Nagel (1974)

Wide Content see **Broad Content**

Will, The: in **modern philosophy**, the faculty of **mind** responsible for decision, choice and **action** initiation. Individual **volitions** were thought to be causes of movements of both the body and the soul. This created two problems (anticipated in **ancient** and **medieval philosophy**). The will as a force directing **passions** to the service of intellect posed the problem of understanding why people sometimes fail to act out of their best judgements (*akrasia* or weakness of the will). And causal **determinism** posed the problem of *free will*. **Hume**'s sceptical view of reason as the slave of passions received a metaphysical expression in the *voluntarism* of Arthur Schopenhauer (1788–1860) who identified the will with the basic force operating throughout nature ('man can do what he wills, but he cannot will what he wills'). With the rejection of Cartesian **dualism** with its notions of the **self** and the *conscious* will there arises the problem of **epiphenomenalism** about **consciousness**. Benjamin Libet's timing studies show that neural events identified with the initiation of an action (moving one's wrist or making a forced choice) precede conscious awareness of the corresponding **intention** or thought by about 350 milliseconds. This makes conscious voluntary action unconsciously initiated: does it make consciousness epiphenomenal? is consciousness causally relevant only after the event, 'training' the **unconscious** mind? is 'free conscious will' manifested in our ability to 'veto' the unconsciously initiated actions (Libet's view)? why and how do we have the subjective feeling of **agency** in our **self-consciousness**?

Further reading: Libet (2004); Wegner (2002)

Williams Syndrome: a genetic disorder marked by significant mental retardation. People with Williams syndrome have impaired arithmetic, visuo-spatial, problem-solving and theoretical reasoning abilities. However, they retain high linguistic (perfect syntax) and **theory of mind** abilities (routinely passing false-belief tests).

Wittgenstein, Ludwig (1889–1951): Austrian philosopher, a major proponent of **logical behaviourism**. In his late philosophy, noticing the heterogeneity in our use of words (the 'language games' we play), he questioned the power of words to correspond to anything, especially private **sensations**. Saying that they are in **pain**, a person cannot be reporting a purely private state because they use a word of a public language. But if they privately decided to give their sensation a name P using an ostensive definition 'this is P', they would not introduce a word of their private language because they would fail to specify a rule for using the word correctly on later occasions (*private language argument*). Reports of **mental states** are not real reports capable of truth or falsity, but *avowals*, pieces of linguistic behaviour that people are disposed to manifest in various situations. **Kripke** emphasises that Wittgenstein's argument raises general **scepticism** about *rule-following*: if the meaning of a word is something that determines its correct application in novel situations, then by defining a word's meaning on the basis of its past uses one will come up with different prescriptions for its future use. Thus there are no internal criteria determining the meaning of a word (or the **content** of a **concept**). These considerations underlie Wittgenstein's view that meaning is use, that the application of a word like 'game' to different realities is guided by unspecific *family resemblances* rather than a single common property, and that linguistic behaviour is nothing other than a form of life.

Further reading: Wittgenstein (1953); Kripke (1982)

Wundt, Wilhelm (1832–1920): German philosopher, the founder of **introspective psychology** and the first psychological laboratory (Leipzig, 1875). Wundt endorsed **parallelism** and **panpsychism,** but he also believed that psychological phenomena can be experimentally studied by controlled **introspection** (observation of one's mental experiences in response to the application of variable sensory stimuli).

Zombies: beings physically identical to humans but lacking **phenomenal consciousness.** If we can imagine them without any contradiction, they are conceivable and thus possible. David Chalmers recently resurrected the zombie idea as an argument against **physicalism** intended to show that the identity of **mental states** with **brain** states cannot be necessary because there is no a priori entailment from physical to **phenomenal** facts. Critics question the move from conceivability to possibility or address the special nature of **phenomenal concepts.**

Bibliography

Useful collections

Block, N. (ed.) (1980), *Readings in the Philosophy of Psychology*, 2 volumes, Cambridge, MA: Harvard University Press.

Chalmers, D. J. (ed.) (2002), *Philosophy of Mind: Classical and Contemporary Readings*, Oxford: Oxford University Press.

Cummins, R. and D. D. Cummins (eds) (2000), *Minds, Brains and Computers: The Foundations of Cognitive Science, An Anthology*, Oxford: Blackwell.

Heil, J. (2004), *Philosophy of Mind: A Guide and An Anthology*, Oxford: Oxford University Press.

Lycan, W. (ed.) (1990), *Mind and Cognition: A Reader*, Oxford: Blackwell.

Lycan, W. (ed.) (1999), *Mind and Cognition: An Anthology*, Oxford: Blackwell.

O'Connor, T. (2003), *Philosophy of Mind: Contemporary Readings*, London: Routledge.

Rosenthal, D. M. (ed.) (1991), *The Nature of Mind*, Oxford: Oxford University Press.

Some useful companions and textbooks

Botterill, G. and P. Carruthers (1999), *Philosophy of Psychology*, Cambridge: Cambridge University Press.

Braddon-Mitchell, D. and F. Jackson (1996), *Philosophy of Mind and Cognition*, Oxford: Blackwell.

Guttenplan, S. (ed.) (1994), *A Companion to the Philosophy of Mind*, Oxford: Blackwell.

Heil, J. (2004), *Philosophy of Mind: A Contemporary Introduction*, 2nd edn, London: Routledge.

Kim, J. (2005), *Philosophy of Mind*, 2nd edn, Boulder, CO: Westview Press.

Rey, G. (1997), *Contemporary Philosophy of Mind: A Contentiously Classical Approach*, New York: Blackwell.
Stich, S. and T. Warfield (eds) (2003), *Blackwell Guide to Philosophy of Mind*, Oxford: Blackwell.

Some useful websites

David Chalmers' Annotated Bibliography of the Philosophy of Mind: http://consc.net/biblio.html
Chris Eliasmith's Dictionary of Philosophy of Mind: http://philosophy. uwaterloo.ca/MindDict
A Field Guide to the Philosophy of Mind: http://host.uniroma3.it/ progetti/kant/field
Stanford Encyclopedia of Philosophy: http://plato.stanford.edu

Bibliography

Allen, C. and M. Bekoff (1997), *Species of Mind: The Philosophy and Biology of Cognitive Ethology*, Cambridge, MA: MIT Press.
Annas, J. (1992), *Hellenistic Philosophy of Mind*, Berkeley, CA: University of California Press.
Anscombe, G. E. M. (1957), *Intention*, Oxford: Blackwell.
Aquinas, St Thomas (2001), *Aquinas's Shorter Summa: Saint Thomas's Own Concise Version of His Summa Theologica*, Sophia: Sophia Institute Press.
Aristotle (1984), *The Complete Works of Aristotle*, Princeton, NJ: Princeton University Press.
Armstrong, D. M. (1968), *A Materialist Theory of the Mind*, London: Routledge & Kegan Paul, Humanities Press.
Armstrong, D. M. (1989), *Universals: An Opinionated Introduction*, Boulder, CO: Westview Press.
Armstrong, D. M., C. B. Martin and U. T. Place (1996), *Dispositions: A Debate*, ed. T. Crane, London: Routledge.
Austin, J. L. (1962), *Sense and Sensibilia*, London: Oxford University Press.
Avramides, A. (2001), *Other Minds*, London: Routledge.
Ayer, A. J. (ed.) (1959), *Logical Positivism*, New York: Free Press.
Baars, B. (1988), *A Cognitive Theory of Consciousness*, Cambridge: Cambridge University Press.
Ballard, D. H., M. M. Hayhoe, P. K. Pook and R. P. N. Rao (1997), 'Deictic codes for the embodiment of cognition', *Behavioral and Brain Sciences*, 20, 723–61.

Barsalou, L. W. (1999), 'Perceptual symbol systems', *Behavioral and Brain Sciences*, 22, 577–633.

Bear, M. F., B. W. Connors and M. A. Paradiso (2001), *Neuroscience: Exploring the Brain*, 2nd edn, Baltimore: Lippincott Williams & Wilkins.

Bechtel, W. and G. Graham (eds) (1998), *A Companion to Cognitive Science*, Malden, MA: Blackwell.

Berkeley, G. (1975), *Philosophical Works*, ed. M. R. Ayers, London: Guernsey Press.

Bermúdez, J. L. (1998), *The Paradox of Self-Consciousness*, Cambridge, MA: MIT Press.

Bickle, J. (1998), *Psychoneural Reduction: The New Wave*, Cambridge, MA: MIT Press.

Block, N. (1978), 'Troubles with functionalism', in C. W. Savage (ed.), *Minnesota Studies in the Philosophy of Science*, vol. 9, Minneapolis: University of Minnesota Press, pp. 261–325.

Block, N. (1986), 'Advertisement for a semantics for psychology', in P. A. French, T. E. Uehling, Jr and H. K. Wettstein (eds), *Midwest Studies in Philosophy*, vol. 10, Minneapolis, MN: University of Minnesota Press, pp. 615–78.

Block, N. (1990), 'Inverted Earth', in J. Tomberlin (ed.), *Philosophical Perspectives*, vol. 4, Atascadero, CA: Ridgeview, pp. 53–79.

Block, N. (1995a), 'On a confusion about a function of consciousness', *Behavioral and Brain Sciences*, 18, 227–87.

Block, N. (1995b), 'The mind as the software of the brain', in E. E. Smith and D. L. Osherson (eds), *An Invitation to Cognitive Science*, 2nd edn, vol. 3, *Thinking*, Cambridge, MA: MIT Press, pp. 377–424.

Block, N. (1997), 'Anti-reductionism slaps back' in J. E. Tomberlin (ed.), *Philosophical Perspectives*, vol. 11, *Mind, Causation, World*, Oxford: Blackwell, pp. 107–33.

Block, N. and J. A. Fodor (1972), 'What psychological states are not', *Philosophical Review*, 81, 159–81.

Boden, M. (2003), *The Creative Mind: Myths and Mechanisms*, 2nd edn, London: Routledge.

Braddon-Mitchell, D. and F. Jackson (1996), *Philosophy of Mind and Cognition*, Oxford: Blackwell.

Brentano, F. [1874] (1973), *Psychology from an Empirical Standpoint*, trans. T. Rancurello, D. Terrell and L. McAllister, London: Routledge & Kegan Paul.

Broad, C. D. [1925] (1976), *The Mind and Its Place in Nature*, London: Routledge & Kegan Paul.

Brooks, R. A. (1991), 'Intelligence without representation', *Artificial Intelligence*, 47, 139–59.

Burge, T. (1979), 'Individualism and the mental', in P. A. French, T. E. Uehling, Jr and H. K. Wettstein (eds), *Midwest Studies in Philosophy*, vol. 4, Minneapolis, MN: University of Minnesota Press, pp. 73–121.

Burge, T. (1986), 'Individualism and psychology', *Philosophical Review*, 95, 3–45.

Carnap, R. (1947), *Meaning and Necessity*, Chicago: Phoenix Books, University of Chicago Press.

Carruthers, P. (2000), *Phenomenal Consciousness*, Cambridge: Cambridge University Press.

Carruthers, P. and J. Boucher (eds) (1998), *Language and Thought*, Cambridge: Cambridge University Press.

Carruthers, P. and P. K. Smith (eds) (1996), *Theories of Theories of Mind*, Cambridge: Cambridge University Press.

Carruthers, P., S. Laurence and S. Stich (eds) (2005), *The Innate Mind: Structure and Contents*, Oxford: Oxford University Press.

Chalmers, D. J. (1996), *The Conscious Mind*, Oxford: Oxford University Press.

Chalmers, D. J. (1999), 'Materialism and the metaphysics of modality', *Philosophy and Phenomenological Research*, 59, 473–93.

Chalmers, D. J. (2004), 'The representational character of experience', in B. Leiter (ed.), *The Future for Philosophy*, Oxford: Oxford University Press, pp. 153–81.

Chisholm, R. (1957), *Perceiving: A Philosophical Study*, Ithaca, NY: Cornell University Press.

Chomsky, N. (2000), *New Horizons in the Study of Language and Mind*, Cambridge, MA: MIT Press.

Churchland, P. M. (1981), 'Eliminative materialism and the propositional attitudes', *Journal of Philosophy*, 78, 67–90.

Churchland, P. M. (1995), *The Engine of Reason, the Seat of the Soul*, Cambridge, MA: MIT Press.

Churchland, P. M. and P. S. Churchland (1998), *On the Contrary: Critical Essays*, Cambridge, MA: MIT Press.

Churchland, P. S. (1986), *Neurophilosophy: Toward a Unified Science of the Mind-Brain*, Cambridge, MA: MIT Press.

Clark, A. (1997), *Being There: Putting Brain, Body and World Together Again*, Cambridge, MA: MIT Press.

Cleeremans, A. (ed.) (2003), *The Unity of Consciousness*, Oxford: Oxford University Press.

Cosmides, L. and J. Tooby (1992), *The Adapted Mind*, Oxford: Oxford University Press.

Cowie, F. (1998), *What's Within? Nativism Reconsidered*, Oxford: Oxford University Press.

Damasio, A. (1999), *The Feeling of What Happens: Body and Emotion in the Making of Consciousness,* New York: Harcourt Brace.

Davidson, D. (1970), 'Mental events', in L. Foster and J. W. Swanson (eds), *Experience and Theory*, Amherst, MA: University of Massachusetts Press, pp. 79–101.

Davidson, D. (1980), *Essays on Actions and Events*, Oxford: Clarendon Press.

Davidson, D. (1984), *Inquiries into Truth and Interpretation*, Oxford: Clarendon Press.

Davidson, D. (1987), 'Knowing one's own mind', *Proceedings and Addresses of the American Philosophical Association*, 60, 441–58.

Dennett, D. C. (1987), *The Intentional Stance*, Cambridge, MA: MIT Press.

Dennett, D. C. (1991), *Consciousness Explained*, Boston: Little, Brown.

Dennett, D. C. (1995), *Darwin's Dangerous Idea: Evolution and the Meanings of Life*, New York: Simon & Schuster.

Dennett, D. C. (2005), *Sweet Dreams: Philosophical Obstacles to a Science of Consciousness*, Cambridge, MA: MIT Press.

Descartes, R. (1984–5), *The Philosophical Writings of Descartes*, 2 vols, eds and trans. J. Cottinghman, R. Stoothoff and D. Murdoch, Cambridge: Cambridge University Press.

Dietrich, E. and A. B. Markman (2003), 'Discrete thoughts: why cognition must use discrete representations', *Mind and Language*, 18, 95–119.

Dretske, F. (1981), *Knowledge and the Flow of Information*, Cambridge, MA: MIT Press.

Dretske, F. (1995), *Naturalizing the Mind*, Cambridge, MA: MIT Press.

Dretske, F. (2000), *Perception, Knowledge and Belief: Selected Essays*, Cambridge: Cambridge University Press.

Edelman, G. M. (1987), *Neural Darwinism: The Theory of Neuronal Group Selection*, New York: Basic Books.

Elman, J. L., E. A. Bates, M. H. Johnson, A. Karmiloff-Smith, D. Parisi and K. Plunkett (1996), *Rethinking Innateness: A Connectionist Perspective on Development*, Cambridge, MA: MIT Press.

Evans, G. (1982), *The Varieties of Reference*, Oxford: Oxford University Press.

Feigl, H. (1958), 'The "mental" and the "physical"', in H. Feigl, M. Scriven and G. Maxwell (eds), *Concepts, Theories and the Mind–Body Problem*, Minnesota Studies in the Philosophy of Science, vol. 2, Minneapolis, MN: University of Minnesota Press, pp. 370–497.

Fodor, J. A. (1974), 'Special sciences', *Synthese*, 28, 97–115.

Fodor, J. A. (1975), *The Language of Thought*, New York: Crowell.

Fodor, J. A. (1980), 'Methodological solipsism considered as a research strategy in cognitive psychology', *Behavioral and Brain Sciences*, 3, 63–72.

Fodor, J. A. (1983), *The Modularity of Mind*, Cambridge, MA: MIT Press.

Fodor, J. A. (1987), *Psychosemantics: The Problem of Meaning in the Philosophy of Mind*, Cambridge, MA: MIT Press.

Fodor, J. A. (1989), 'Making mind matter more', *Philosophical Topics*, 67, 59–79.

Fodor, J. A. (2000), *The Mind Doesn't Work That Way: The Scope and Limits of Computational Psychology*, Cambridge, MA: MIT Press.

Fodor, J. A. (2003), *Hume Variations*, Oxford: Clarendon Press.

Fodor, J. A. and E. Lepore (1992), *Holism: A Shopper's Guide*, Oxford: Blackwell.

Fodor, J. A. and Z. Pylyshyn (1988), 'Connectionism and cognitive architecture: a critical analysis', *Cognition*, 28, 3–71.

Foster, J. (1996), *The Immaterial Self: A Defence of the Cartesian Dualist Conception of the Mind*, London: Routledge.

Frege, G. (1960), *Translations from the Philosophical Writings of Gottlob Frege*, eds P. Geach and M. Black, Oxford: Oxford University Press.

Freud, S. (1962), *The Ego and the Id*, trans. J. Strachey, London and New York: W. W. Norton.

Gendler Szabo, T. and J. Hawthorne (eds) (2006), *Perceptual Experience*, Oxford: Oxford University Press.

Gettier, E. (1963), 'Is justified true belief knowledge?', *Analysis*, 23, 121–3.

Gibson, J. J. (1979), *The Ecological Approach to Visual Perception*, Boston: Houghton Mifflin.

Gigerenzer, G., P. Todd and the ABC Research Group (1999), *Simple Heuristics that Make Us Smart*, Oxford: Oxford University Press.

Gillett, C. and B. Loewer (2001), *Physicalism and its Discontents*, Cambridge: Cambridge University Press.

Goodale, M. A. and A. D. Milner (2005), *Sight Unseen: An Exploration of Conscious and Unconscious Vision*, Oxford: Oxford University Press.

Gould, S. J. and R. Lewontin (1979), 'The spandrels of San Marco and the Panglossian paradigm: a critique of the adaptationist programme', *Proceedings of the Royal Society*, B205, 581–98.

Grice, H. P. (1957), 'Meaning', in *Studies in the Way of Words* (1989), Cambridge, MA: Harvard University Press, pp. 213–23.

Gunther, Y. H. (ed.) (2003), *Essays in Nonconceptual Content*, Cambridge, MA: MIT Press.

Hardin, C. L. (1993), *Color for Philosophers: Unweaving the Rainbow*, expanded edition, Indianapolis, IN: Hackett.

Harman, G. (1987), '(Non-solipsistic) conceptual role semantics', in E. Lepore (ed.), *New Directions in Semantics*, London: Academic Press, pp. 55–81.

Harnad, S. (1990), 'The symbol grounding problem', *Physica D*, 42, 335–46.

Hauser, D. M., N. Chomsky and W. T. Fitch (2002), 'The faculty of language: what is it, who has it, and how did it evolve?', *Science*, 298, 22 November, 1569–79.

Hebb, D. O. (1949), *The Organisation of Behaviour: A Neuropsychological Theory*, New York: Wiley.

Heil, J. and A. Mele (eds) (1993), *Mental Causation*, Oxford: Clarendon Press.

Hobbes, T. [1651] (1957), *Leviathan*, Oxford: Oxford University Press.

Horgan, T. and J. Tienson (2002), 'The intentionality of phenomenology and the phenomenology of intentionality', in D. Chalmers (ed.), *Philosophy of Mind: Classical and Contemporary Readings*, Oxford: Oxford University Press, pp. 520–33.

Hume, D. [1748] (1994), *An Enquiry Concerning Human Understanding*, ed. A. Flew, La Salle, IL: Open Court.

Hurley, S. (1998), *Consciousness in Action*, Cambridge, MA: Harvard University Press.

Husserl, E. [1913] (1982), *Ideas Pertaining to a Pure Phenomenology and to a Phenomenological Philosophy, First Book*, trans. F. Kersten, Dordrecht: Kluwer Academic Publishers.

Huxley, T. H. (2001), *Man's Place in Nature*, ed. S. G. Gould, New York: Modern Library.

Jackson, F. C. (1977), *Perception: A Representative Theory*, Cambridge: Cambridge University Press.

Jackson, F. C. (1982), 'Epiphenomenal qualia', *Philosophical Quarterly*, 32, 127–36.

Jackson, F. C. (1993), 'Armchair metaphysics', in J. Hawthorne and M. Michael (eds), *Philosophy in Mind: The Place of Philosophy in the Study of Mind*, Dordrecht: Kluwer Academic, pp. 23–42.

Jackson, F. C. (2004), 'Mind and illusion', in P. Ludlow, Y. Nagasawa and D. Stoljar (eds), *There's Something about Mary: Essays on Phenomenal Consciousness and Frank Jackson's Knowledge Argument*, Cambridge, MA: MIT Press, pp. 421–42.

James, W. [1890] (1981), *The Principles of Psychology*, Cambridge, MA: Harvard University Press.

James, W. [1912] (1976), *Essays in Radical Empiricism*, Cambridge, MA: Harvard University Press.

Kant, I. [1781] (1997), *The Critique of Pure Reason*, Cambridge: Cambridge University Press.

Keil, F. (1989), *Concepts, Kinds and Cognitive Development*, Cambridge, MA: MIT Press.

Kim, J. (1993), *Supervenience and Mind*, Cambridge: Cambridge University Press.

Kim, J. (2002), 'Precis of *Mind in a Physical World*' followed by Peer Reviews, *Philosophy and Phenomenological Research*, 65, 640–80.

Kim, J. (2005), *Physicalism or Something Near Enough*, Princeton, NJ: Princeton University Press.

Koch, C. (2004), *The Quest for Consciousness: A Neurobiological Approach*, Englewood, CO: Roberts.

Kripke, S. (1980), *Naming and Necessity*, Oxford: Blackwell.

Kripke, S. (1982), *Wittgenstein: On Rules and Private Language*, Oxford: Basil Blackwell.

Leibniz, G. W. [1714] (1989), *Principles of Philosophy, or, The Monadology*, in *Philosophical Essays*, Indianapolis, IN: Hackett.

Lepore, E. and B. Loewer (1989), 'More on making mind matter', *Philosophical Topics*, 27, 175–91.

Lepore, E. and R. Van Gulick (eds) (1991), *John Searle and His Critics*, Oxford: Blackwell.

Levine, J. (1983), 'Materialism and qualia: the explanatory gap', *Pacific Philosophical Quarterly*, 64, 354–61.

Lewis, D. (1972), 'Psychophysical and theoretical identifications', *Australasian Journal of Philosophy*, 50, 249–58.

Lewis, D. (1980), 'Mad pain and Martian pain', in N. Block (ed.), *Readings in the Philosophy of Psychology*, vol. 1, Cambridge, MA: Harvard University Press, pp. 216–22.

Lewis, D. (1988), 'What experience teaches', in J. Copley-Coltheart (ed.), *Proceedings of the Russellian Society*, vol. 13, Sydney: University of Sydney, pp. 29–57.

Lewis, D. (1994), 'Reduction of mind', in S. Guttenplan (ed.), *A Companion to the Philosophy of Mind*, Oxford: Blackwell.

Lewis, M. and J. M. Haviland-Jones (eds) (2000), *Handbook of Emotions*, New York: Guilford Press.

Libet, B. (2004), *Mind Time: The Temporal Factor in Consciousness*, Cambridge, MA: Harvard University Press.

Loar, B. (1997), 'Phenomenal states', second version, in N. Block, O. Flanagan and Güzeldere (eds), *The Nature of Consciousness: Philosophical Debates*, Cambridge, MA: MIT Press, pp. 597–616.

Locke, J. [1689] (1975), *An Essay Concerning Human Understanding*, ed. P. H. Nidditch, Oxford: Clarendon Press.

Ludlow, P. and N. Martin (1998), *Externalism and Self-Knowledge*, Stanford, CA: CSLI Publications.

Ludlow, P., Y. Nagasawa and D. Stoljar (eds) (2004), *There's Something about Mary: Essays on Phenomenal Consciousness and Frank Jackson's Knowledge Argument*, Cambridge, MA: MIT Press.

Lycan, W. G. (1987), *Consciousness*, Cambridge, MA: MIT Press.

Lycan, W. G. (1996), *Consciousness and Experience*, Cambridge, MA: MIT Press.

Malebranche, N. [1674–5] (1997), *Nicolas Malebranche: The Search after Truth and Elucidations*, trans. T. M. Lennon and P. J. Olscamp, Cambridge: Cambridge University Press.

Margolis, E. and S. Laurence (eds) (1999), *Concepts: Core Readings*, Cambridge, MA: MIT Press.

Marr, D. (1982), *Vision*, San Francisco: Freeman.

Martin, M. G. F. (2004), 'The limits of self-awareness', *Philosophical Studies*, 120, 37–89.

McDowell, J. (1994), *Mind and World*, Cambridge, MA: Harvard University Press.

McGinn, C. (1989), 'Can we solve the mind–body problem?', *Mind*, 98, 349–66.

McGinn, C. (1991), *Ten Problems of Consciousness*, Oxford: Blackwell.

Mele, A. R. (ed.) (1997), *The Philosophy of Action*, Oxford: Oxford University Press.

Mele, A. R. (2001), *Self-Deception Unmasked*, Princeton, NJ: Princeton University Press.

Mele, A. R. and P. Rawling (eds) (2004), *The Oxford Handbook of Rationality*, Oxford: Oxford University Press.

Merleau-Ponty, M. [1945] (1962), *Phenomenology of Perception*, trans. C. Smith, New York: Humanities Press.

Metzinger, T. (2003), *Being No One: The Self-Model of Subjectivity*, Cambridge, MA: MIT Press.

Mill, J. S. [1843] (2002), *A System of Logic: Ratiocinative and Inductive*, Honolulu, HI: University Press of the Pacific.

Millikan, R. G. (1984), *Language, Thought and Other Biological Categories*, Cambridge, MA: MIT Press.

Millikan, R. G. (2000), *On Clear and Confused Ideas*, Cambridge: Cambridge University Press.

Minsky, M. (forthcoming), *The Emotion Machine*, New York: Simon & Schuster.

Murphy, G. L. (2002), *The Big Book of Concepts*, Cambridge, MA: MIT Press.

Nagel, E. (1961), *The Structure of Science*, New York: Harcourt, Brace, and World.

Nagel, T. (1971), 'Brain bisection and the unity of consciousness', *Synthese*, 22, 396–413.

Nagel, T. (1974), 'What is it like to be a bat', *Philosophical Review*, 83, 435–50.

Noë, A. and E. T. Thompson (eds) (2002), *Vision and Mind*, Cambridge, MA: MIT Press.

Ockham (1990), *Philosophical Writings*, ed. and trans. P. Boehner, Indianapolis, IN: Hackett.

Olson, E. (1997), *The Human Animal: Personal Identity Without Psychology*, Oxford: Oxford University Press.

O'Regan, J. K. and A. Noë (2001), 'A sensorimotor account of vision and visual consciousness', *Behavioral and Brain Sciences*, 24, 939–1031.

Papineau, D. (1993), *Philosophical Naturalism*, Oxford: Blackwell.

Papineau, D. (2002), *Thinking about Consciousness*, Oxford: Clarendon Press.

Parfit, D. (1984), *Reasons and Persons*, Oxford: Oxford University Press.

Pasnau, R. (1997), *Theories of Cognition in the Later Middle Ages*, Cambridge: Cambridge University Press.

Peacocke, C. (1992), *A Study of Concepts*, Cambridge, MA: MIT Press.

Peirce, C. S. (1992), *The Essential Peirce: Selected Philosophical Writings*, ed. C. Kloesel, Bloomington, IN: Indiana University Press.

Penrose, R. (1994), *Shadows of the Mind: A Search for the Missing Science of Consciousness*, Oxford: Oxford University Press.

Perring, C. (1997), 'Degrees of personhood', *Journal of Medicine and Philosophy*, 22, 173–7.

Pessin, A., S. Goldberg and H. Putnam (eds) (1996), *The Twin Earth Chronicles: Twenty Years of Reflection on Hilary Putnam's 'The Meaning of Meaning'*, Armonk, NY: M. E. Sharpe.

Pinker, S. (2002), *The Blank Slate: The Modern Denial of Human Nature*, New York: Viking.

Place, U. T. (1956), 'Is consciousness a brain process?', *British Journal of Psychology*, 45, 243–55.

Plato (1989), *The Collected Dialogues of Plato*, Princeton, NJ: Princeton University Press.

Preston, J. and M. Bishop (eds) (2002), *Views in the Chinese Room: New Essays on Searle and Artificial Intelligence*, New York: Oxford University Press.

Putnam, H. (1967), 'Psychological predicates' (reprinted as 'The nature of mental states' in some collections), in W. H. Capitan and D. D. Merrill (eds), *Art, Mind and Religion*, Pittsburgh: University of Pittsburgh Press, pp. 37–48.

Putnam, H. (1968), 'Brains and behavior', in R. J. Butler (ed.), *Analytical Philosophy*, vol. 2, Oxford: Oxford: University Press, pp. 1–19.

Putnam, H. (1975), 'The meaning of meaning', in *Mind, Language and Reality: Philosophical Papers*, Cambridge: Cambridge University Press, pp. 215–71.

Putnam, H. (1981), *Reason, Truth and History*, Cambridge: Cambridge University Press.

Putnam, H. (1988), *Representation and Reality*, Cambridge, MA: MIT Press.

Putnam, H. (2000), *The Threefold Cord*, New York: Columbia University Press.

Pylyshyn, Z. W. (1984), *Computation and Cognition*, Cambridge, MA: MIT Press.

Pylyshyn, Z. W. (2003), *Seeing and Visualizing*, Cambridge, MA: MIT Press.

Quartz, S. R. and T. J. Sejnowski (1997), 'The neural basis of cognitive development: a constructivist manifesto', *Behavioral and Brain Sciences*, 20, 537–96.

Quine, W. V. O. (1953), 'Two dogmas of empiricism', in *From a Logical Point of View*, Cambridge, MA: Harvard University Press, pp. 20–46.

Quine, W. V. O. (1960), *Word and Object*, Cambridge, MA: MIT Press.

Quine, W. V. O. (1969), *Ontological Relativity and Other Essays*, New York: Columbia University Press.

Rosenberg, G. (2004), *A Place for Consciousness: Probing the Deep Structure of the Natural World*, Oxford: Oxford University Press.

Rosenthal, D. M. (1986), 'Two concepts of consciousness', *Philosophical Studies*, 49, 329–59.

Rumelhart, D. E. and J. L. McClelland (eds) (1986), *Parallel Distributed Processing: Explorations in the Microstructure of Cognition*, 2 vols, Cambridge, MA: MIT Press.

Russell, B. (1956), *Logic and Knowledge*, ed. R. C. Marsh, London and New York: Routledge.

Ryle, G. (1949), *The Concept of Mind*, London: Hutchinson.

Samuels, R. (2000), 'Massively modular minds: evolutionary psychology and cognitive architecture', in P. Carruthers and A. Chamberlain (eds), *Evolution and the Human Mind: Modularity, Language and Meta-Cognition*, Cambridge: Cambridge University Press.

Sartre, J.-P. [1943] (1948), *Being and Nothingness*, trans. H. E. Barnes, New York: Philosophical Library.

Savage-Rumbaugh, S., S. G. Shaker and T. J. Taylor (1998), *Apes, Language and the Human Mind*, New York: Oxford University Press.

Searle, J. R. (1980), 'Minds, brains and programs', *Behavioral and Brain Sciences*, 3, 417–24.

Searle, J. R. (1983), *Intentionality*, Cambridge: Cambridge University Press.

Searle, J. R. (1992), *The Rediscovery of Mind*, Cambridge, MA: MIT Press.

Segal, G. (2000), *A Slim Book about Narrow Content*, Cambridge, MA: MIT Press.

Sellars, W. (1963), *Science, Perception and Reality*, London: Routledge & Kegan Paul.

Shoemaker, S. (1994), 'Self-knowledge and "inner sense"', *Philosophy and Phenomenological Research*, 65, 576–603.

Siewert, C. (1998), *The Significance of Consciousness*, Princeton, NJ: Princeton University Press.

Smart, J. J. C. (1959), 'Sensations and brain processes', *Philosophical Review*, 68, 141–56.

Smith, A. D. (2000), 'Space and sight', *Mind*, 109, 481–518.

Smith, A. D. (2002), *The Problem of Perception*, Cambridge, MA: Harvard University Press.

Smith, E. E. and D. L. Osherson (eds) (1995), *An Invitation to Cognitive Science*, 2nd edn, vol. 3 *Thinking*, Cambridge, MA: MIT Press.

Smith, Q. and A. Jokic (eds) (2003), *Consciousness: New Philosophical Essays*, Oxford: Oxford University Press.

Spelke, E. (1990), 'Principles of object perception', *Cognitive Science*, 14, 29–56.

Spinoza, B. (1994), *A Spinoza Reader: The Ethics and Other Works*, Princeton, NJ: Princeton University Press.

Stanley, J. and T. Williamson (2001), 'Knowing how', *Journal of Philosophy*, 98, 411–44.

Sterelny, K. (1983), 'Natural kind terms', *Pacific Philosophical Quarterly*, 64, 110–25.

Sterelny, K. (1990), *The Representational Theory of Mind: An Introduction*, Oxford: Blackwell.

Stich, S. (1983), *From Folk Psychology to Cognitive Science*, Cambridge, MA: MIT Press.

Stich, S. (1996), *Deconstructing the Mind*, Oxford: Oxford University Press.

Strawson, P. F. (1959), *Individuals*, London: Methuen.

Thompson, E. (1995), *Colour Vision*, London: Routledge.

Turing, A. M. (1950), 'Computing machinery and intelligence', *Mind*, 59, 433–60.

Tye, M. (1989). *The Metaphysics of Mind*, Cambridge: Cambridge University Press.

Tye, M. (1995), *Ten Problems of Consciousness: A Representational Theory of the Phenomenal Mind*, Cambridge, MA: MIT Press.

van Gelder, T. (1998), 'The dynamical hypothesis in cognitive science', *Behavioral and Brain Sciences*, 21, 615–65.

Wade, N. J. (2004), *Perception and Illusion: Historical Perspectives*, New York: Springer.

Walter, S. and H.-D. Heckmann (2003), *Physicalism and Mental Causation*, Thorverton: Imprint Academic.

Watson, J. B. (1925), *Behaviorism*, New York: W. W. Norton.

Wegner, D. M. (2002), *The Illusion of Conscious Will*, Cambridge, MA: MIT Press.

Williamson, T. (2000), *Knowledge and Its Limits*, Oxford: Oxford University Press.

Wittgenstein, L. (1953), *Philosophical Investigations*, trans. G. E. M. Anscombe, Oxford: Basil Blackwell.